HENRY JAMES
AND H. G. WELLS

HENRY JAMES, *c.* 1900

H. G. WELLS, 1901

HENRY JAMES

AND

H. G. WELLS

*A Record of their Friendship,
their Debate on the Art of Fiction,
and their Quarrel*

Edited with an Introduction by
Leon Edel & Gordon N. Ray

London
RUPERT HART-DAVIS
1958

808·3

E14,638

ED 2

Printed in Great Britain by Richard Clay and Company, Ltd.,
Bungay, Suffolk

CONTENTS

FOREWORD

In this volume will be found the record of an historic disagreement between two famous novelists. They fell out —as novelists will—about the purpose and practice of their craft. Both were gifted men, both could give extraordinary utterance to their beliefs, and their dispute inevitably attracted wide attention. It began as an amicable and private dialogue on Olympus, but its ending was not without a note of high drama, for one of the novelists lost his temper. "Leviathan retrieving pebbles . . . a magnificent but painful hippopotamus resolved at any cost, even at the cost of its dignity, upon picking up a pea," wrote H. G. Wells of Henry James's elaborations of the art of fiction. To which James replied: "It is art that *makes* life, makes interest, makes importance. . . . I know of no substitute whatever for the force and beauty of its process."

The general outline of the strange literary exchange between James, one of the great architects and builders of the modern novel, and Wells, a creator of "science fiction" and a prophet of world organization, has been familiar ever since 1920, when Percy Lubbock published its final epistolary record in *The Letters of Henry James*. More than a decade later Wells offered in his *Experiment in Autobiography* his understandably biased view of James and his work, without however making direct allusion to the way in which he had lampooned and parodied the older novelist. More recently Michael Swan, whose devotion to James perhaps exceeds his devotion to historical fact, culled certain paragraphs from the unpublished letters and by stringing these together tried to suggest an elementary psychological solution to the quarrel—that Wells had imaged James as a sort of angry father and that his derision at the end was nothing more than the revolt of a son against a formidable parent.

But this was a Freudian guess about a matter which cannot be so simply explained, as may be seen from the full documentation which is provided for the first time in this book. We have printed all the extant letters exchanged by James and Wells, together with articles which took their private debate into the public arena—and served also to exacerbate their mutual irritation—and we have added the passages in Wells's autobiography in which his side of the case was offered to the public after James's death. It is essential that their correspondence thus be read in the context of its surrounding documents, both because of the intrinsic importance of these statements and because of disproportion in the surviving letters. The bachelor American novelist liked to burn his personal papers; the faithful wife of the English novelist tended to hoard his. Consequently forty-six letters from James to Wells have been preserved, while James saved only eleven from Wells, and these too were intended for ultimate destruction. To complete the record we have also included the seven letters which remain from James to Mrs. Wells.

These materials make possible after nearly half a century a more searching judgment on a debate which, as the late E. K. Brown showed in an illuminating essay, involved in reality "two formulae for fiction." In a sense it involved also two ways of life: the way of the writer like Wells or Bernard Shaw who subordinates his art to his social message, and the way of the dedicated artist like James or Proust for whom art is the only valid means of encompassing and preserving human experience. Wells and Shaw, as socialists, believed in ' *la littérature engagée*,' a useable, functional art appropriate to the new world they wished to fashion out of the old. James wanted art to be neither consciously prophetic nor self-consciously didactic. He preferred to take life as it comes, to deal with it in its *status quo*, with measure, balance, and moderation. There was enough for the artist to do in the act of seeing, feeling, arriving at awareness—and creating from this awareness—without making of his creations instruments for social instruction and guidance. A few years before his trouble with Wells, James quietly and succinctly debated this very question with Shaw. They talked to each other as equals; neither threatened the other's sovereign position, and the correspondence, published in *The Complete Plays of Henry James*, constitutes an admirable—and honourable—statement of their opposing views. In James's much more extensive exchanges with Wells the deeper natures of the two men became involved in a fashion that made the issues between them far more complex and their discussion of these issues far more personal. Only by reading the documents here presented in the light of their contrasting temperaments, can we arrive at a full understanding of the debate. And such an understanding is worth achieving, for by extension into our time the issues touch one of the exposed nerves of our century: the distinction to be drawn between literature as the voice of the individual and literature engaged in the furtherance of social welfare. Thus envisioned the story of James and Wells is a parable of the two great camps into which artists have been divided in the twentieth century.

Though this volume is the first of a number in which selected papers from the H. G. Wells Archive at the University of Illinois will be offered to the public, it happens that most of the letters which we print or quote from are there represented only by photographic reproductions. It is with pleasure, therefore, that we record our gratitude to the holders of the manuscript originals of this correspondence: to Mr. Simon Nowell-Smith for James's letters to the Wellses, and to the Houghton Library of Harvard University (and particularly Professor William A. Jackson) for Wells's letters to James. We are also obliged to the executors of James and Wells for permission to print the copyright and unpublished material in this book. Grants from the Graduate College Research Board of the University of Illinois made possible the sorting and cataloging by Mrs. Charles H. Shattuck of the Wells Archive, a necessary preliminary to the scholarly presentation of this correspondence, as of the others to be included in subsequent volumes.

LEON EDEL
New York University

GORDON N. RAY
University of Illinois

26 *April* 1957

INTRODUCTION

I

HENRY JAMES and H. G. Wells appear to have met in 1898. Three years earlier Wells had witnessed James's public discomfiture at the first night of *Guy Domville*, when the gallery booed the American novelist as he came out to take a bow before a fashionable London audience. The night had been doubly memorable for Wells—it was the night he met Bernard Shaw. Both were present as drama critics, and they walked away from the theatre together at the evening's end.

In 1898 James was fifty-five, Wells thirty-two. The senior writer had recently forsaken London, where he had lived for two decades, and installed himself in Lamb House, Rye, in Sussex, the permanent home he had always wanted, a rural retreat from the pressures of the British capital. He had in recent years gone through a series of personal crises: his plays had failed, his books were not selling, critics praised him but did not understand him, he felt unwanted and his old age seemed to stretch before him, blank and dreary. Yet even at this moment he had written "The Turn of the Screw", which was to give him a momentary "lift," and presently he was to find, in his Rye retreat, leisure for the creation of the three major novels which he wrote after the turn of the

century. The paradox of his life was that, though un-
read, he remained a literary lion. His opinions on the art
of fiction were valued; he was *"cher maître"* to Joseph
Conrad and to his younger contemporaries. He was
established as a great American man of letters who had
chosen England as his home. He was a familiar figure at
the Athenaeum and Reform Clubs; he was cultivated by
hostesses. He had from the first been an urbane gentleman, and he lived in a settled outward security that gave
the world no inkling of his inner battles and his deeply
frustrated sense that his pen had ceased to earn for him
the comfortable margin of his middle years.

Wells, on the other hand, was still a struggling writer,
whose scientific romances, though widely bought and
enjoyed, had as yet attracted only occasional—and often
condescending—notice from established critics of fiction.
He was a young man of the lower middle class, the son of
a lady's-maid and a gardener, hemmed in, with all the
stigmata of his origin still about him, by the rigid social
boundaries of the Victorian world. By origin he belonged, so to speak, "below stairs," but his sharp intelligence and formidable energy, conveyed to the public
by a nimble pen, were allowing him to wander about
increasingly in the drawing-room.

That these two writers should have been drawn together in the world of letters may seem strange. But
James, the saturated cosmopolitan, was dedicated to his
craft above all else, and he attracted young writers to him.

Wells was no exception. James welcomed him as a *confrère* and an equal, insisting only on their difference in age and experience. Wells, who never lost the cockney impudence of his youth, was grateful for this friendship, but he could not accept it without some underlying resentment. First they exchanged letters in which James talked of fictional techniques with that weight of authority which had become second nature to him, and Wells responded in affable politeness and respect, and with a modesty that was to disappear as he grew more sure of himself. In 1900, when Wells moved to Spade House, Sandgate, across Romney Marsh from Rye, the two began to meet with some frequency. They had friends in common—Conrad and Stephen Crane among others. Wells brought Gissing to visit James. They spent long hours in the Lamb House garden or in the library, in endless talk. Their letters on literary subjects may be regarded, indeed, as mere footnotes to their many long conversations at Lamb House. Unfortunately we must content ourselves with the footnotes; there was no Boswell to record the talk. But the warmth and sincerity of their friendship as well as the character of their talk may be deduced from the correspondence.

Years later Wells was to remark, with that shrewdness of insight which makes of his autobiography a remarkable personal record: "I bothered him and he bothered me." The deeper truth of this does not seem to have been apparent to him or James at the time they were seeing

B

each other. The attraction which the alert, sharp mind of the young Wells had for James, and the fascination of the Master for the young man, quite coated over the underlying anxiety each created for the other. James had an easy acceptance of himself and the world; Wells was working hard to make the world accept him. James knew his place and had always known it: he was reconciled to the man-made hierarchies and wielded his pen as if it were a sceptre. Wells carried on his shoulder the invisible chip of inferior social rank in a society where such matters still deeply counted. One suspects that he experienced the American novelist as he experienced the British upper classes: there remained always an underedge of hostility. When he could experience his friendship with James on a footing of equality he was fairly comfortable; but when James criticized his work, there was a certain inner squirming, not because of the criticism *per se*, but because the raw surfaces of old inferiorities and "below-stairs" insecurities were being touched unwittingly by the older artist. The essential difference between the two lay, however, in the fact that Wells's scientific training, combined with his need for self-assertion, made him an exponent of a materialistic kind of artistry to which James was utterly opposed. Wells could not for long accept beauty and art as ends in themselves.

Another way of expressing this fundamental difference is to describe the manner in which they experienced reality. James could look reality full in the face and unabashedly change its form to suit himself: the world was his to refashion into art. Wells also looked reality full in the face, but there the resemblance ended. He saw it with the eye of a statesman or a trade union leader: reality was not something to be submitted to the alchemy of the imagination; it was something to be *manipulated* with all the resources of the human intelligence. We know for instance how James used to look at a building: he studied the colour of its surface, he pondered its relation to the past, its human and its sentimental associations, its uglinesses and its beauties; and because his imagination cherished it for the human qualities it represented, he no more entertained any notion of tearing it down than he would of changing the ordered hierarchies of the world's society. Wells, looking at the same building, would address himself primarily to its human usefulness, with little regard for its associations or aesthetic qualities. If it had none, the only thing to do was to tear it down and put something more functional in its place.

Thus both writers touched deep inner chords within one another, chords of mutual response and of troubled feeling. Below the animated surface of their talk they had to find ways of coping with the anxieties they induced in one another. Wells wanted to forget his origins, the poverty and struggle he had undergone, the battle he had fought to make a place for himself in a hard world, and his way of doing this was to champion plans for altering the world. James, by his very presence and manner, tended to make it difficult for him to forget. On his side, the American novelist was confronted by a man he wanted to accept as an artist—and a gentleman—but he found himself never wholly allowed to do so. Periodically Wells would kick over the traces. He refused to be drawn into James's world: to do so would be to surrender, perhaps, his fighting self and the sovereignty he had sought so hard to win.

II

Small wonder then that this friendship passed through a series of complicated phases. Until 1902 the relationship was clearly that of master and disciple. Wells appreciated the sympathy, interest, encouragement, of a writer whose accomplishment seemed altogether beyond his grasp. But between 1902 and 1905 there was a marked shift. Fame began to come to Wells with tolerable rapidity. James, writing in this period the three major novels of his maturity—*The Ambassadors*, *The Wings of the Dove* and *The Golden Bowl*, found that these works were received with bewilderment when they were not ignored. Wells's public grew; his own, in terms of sales, seemed to be shrinking. This, however, was nothing new in his career. He had watched Kipling leap into fame a decade earlier; he had witnessed the success of Stevenson; he had seen the rise and fall of Oscar Wilde. He had long ago reconciled himself to the anomalies of "success" in the market-place. He rejoiced in the good fortune of his

friends and looked a little ruefully at his dwindling
royalties. In 1903 he writes to Wells (it is ~~probably~~ of *see p.* 88
The Ambassadors), "My book has been out upwards of a
month and, not emulating your 4,000, has sold, I believe,
to the extent of four copies. In America it is doing better
—promises to reach 400." And on November 27 of that
year he spoke of his own "little affairs" as against Wells's
"big interests and big possibilities." In James's view these
"big possibilities" were artistic as well as pecuniary, for *× ho!*
Wells was now not only writing scientific romance, he
was also assuming the role of a critic of society and
essaying the still more difficult role of prophet. Moreover
his fiction was brilliantly mirroring the humours of
lower-middle-class life. When *A Modern Utopia* and
Kipps appeared within a few months of each other in
1905, his central position in the English literary scene
could no longer be denied.

Recognition brought new confidence as well as independence to Wells, and James's letters show a sincere
pleasure in the growth of his young friend's artistic talent.
Between 1905 and 1911 he recognized what critics have
said since his time, that in the Wells of this decade there
appeared the promise of a great comic genius, a twentieth-
century Dickens. "You must at moments," he wrote,
"make dear old Dickens turn—for envy of the eye and
the ear and the nose and the mouth of you—in his
grave." During these years Wells made his most
determined effort to write novels that might have some

claim to permanence. As he sent these one by one to James, he received in return always an elaborate and detailed reply. Unlike other writers, who gracefully acknowledge books sent to them by their *confrères* without feeling impelled to write a full-scale critique of them, James wrote Wells letters which amounted to confidential reviews of his books. Yet the two men were to a certain extent talking at cross purposes. James spoke for the *avant-garde* form of fiction he was creating; Wells accepted the novel as what it had nearly always been in England—an easy-going narrative unconcerned with its *raison d'être*. Moreover, James's letters contained a certain amount of his "mere twaddle of graciousness," as he himself characterised his mandarin politeness, coupled with a cushioning of harsher criticism in fantastic metaphors and polysyllabic ponderosities. "I love your agglomerated lucubrations," James writes, explaining that he doesn't read Wells in the magazines but waits until he appears in book form. "Continue then to agglomerate." To a man as direct and unceremonious as Wells, such epistolary ritualism was sufficiently comical, particularly since he sometimes failed to see that James himself was not always serious. Wells was also very much alive to what he regarded as the comic elements in James's way of life at Lamb House. Like G. K. Chesterton, he found his host "a very stately and courteous old gentleman," who erred perhaps "on the side of solemnity and slowness." In the house of this refined and courtly bachelor

everything was orderly and formal. He regarded himself, Chesterton relates in his *Autobiography*, "as a sort of
steward or custodian of the mysteries and secrets of a
great house, where ghosts might have walked with all
possible propriety. . . . He inhabited the house with all
the gravity and loyalty of the family ghosts; not without
something of the oppressive delicacy of a highly cultured
family butler." This austere setting, and the spectacle of
James, like Sir Charles Grandison, "behaving uniformly
well" within it, supplied a constant temptation to the
mischievous small boy in Wells. During the summer of
1908 Chesterton resided in the house next to James's in
Rye. For some weeks James did not call on his new
neighbour; and Chesterton tells how Wells during this
time of probation, when he could no longer endure
elevated discussion on the art of the novel, used "to make
irreverent darts and dashes through the sombre house and
the sacred garden and drop notes to me over the garden
wall." Wells's ambivalent account of James in his
Experiment in Autobiography is written somewhat in the
spirit of these spurts of naughtiness; even many years
after his friend's death he had not conquered the underlying *malaise* which James's euphemisms and extreme
propriety of manner had inspired in him.

Yet Wells quite clearly recognized James as the master
of his art. He may not have been prepared to learn the
"lesson of the master," but he was more than willing to
listen to him. For instance, an unpublished letter of

19 September 1902 to Arnold Bennett, one of the un-
converted regarding James, reveals him recommending
The Wings of the Dove "as a book to read and learn from.
There are things in it *you* couldn't do, *I* couldn't do,
nobody could do but James. Some are defects—some
aren't. Anyhow I will give an ocean of *Octopuses* and a
bloody suburb of *Houses With the Green Shutters* and all
of George Moore whatsoever for this book."

No doubt James's letters contained much damaging
and unanswerable criticism, despite their verbal cushioning. But they provided at the same time the kind of
comment and appreciation that anyone who has laboured
seriously over a book longs to receive and almost never
does. With his finely attuned literary perceptions and his
subtle mind, James nearly always cut through to the core
of each work. It is characteristic of the American novelist,
for example, that while English reviewers and readers
were exercised over the sexual question in *Ann Veronica*,
he was troubled by something which no one was dis-
cussing. Had Wells dealt adequately with the character
of the heroine and her " projected ego" as it emerges in
the book? James found her wanting in "clearness and
nuances" as a person.

In Wells's non-fictional writings James found an
initial obstacle to appreciation: he insisted upon the un-
bridgeable gap between the artist who attempts to
describe and pass judgment only upon what he knows
and feels intimately, and the sociologist who seeks to fit

society as a whole into his preconceptions. No doubt
Anticipations had a "great source of interest that never
failed; which was simply H.G.W. himself," James wrote,
but "my world is somehow other." He could only regard *Mankind in the Making* as "a record of romantic
adventure of which You are the hero." *A Modern
Utopia* showed him Wells as the personification of
"cheek," and when James repeated this word several
times he must have acutely irritated Wells's sense of
being the "outsider." What James recognized, in these
writings, in his deep psychological awareness of human
motivations and impulses, was the extent to which Wells,
behind the mask of critic and prophet, was portraying
himself in all that he wrote. The issue between them was
underlined clearly in comments they made to one
another about their American books. Wells's *Future in
America* of 1906 and James's *American Scene* of 1907,
published in identical format by Chapman and Hall, represented contrasts that had nothing to do with Wells
being an Englishman and James an American. James
found Wells too simple; Wells replied that James was not
simple enough. James told Wells his "sublime and
heroic cheek" couldn't quite conceal his tendency "always to simplify." Wells on America, James found, was
"too *loud*, as if the country shouted at you, hurrying
past, every hint it had to give and you yelled back your
comment on it." Wells's reply to this was both graceful and penetrating: "You take the whole thing as an

ineffectual civilisation and judge it with so temperate and informed a decisiveness. But I wish there was a Public worthy of you. . . . How much will they get out of what you have got in?" Flattering this was; but it contained also a fund of bitter truth.

In reading Wells's stories, James was able for the most part to forget the sociologist in the writer of fiction. He told Wells that he considered him by far the most interesting novelist of his generation, "in fact, the only interesting one." This, however, did not prevent him from urging upon Wells his own theories of fiction and judging Wells's novels, inevitably, by the light of his own long-established techniques. The rising curve of James's exasperation may be readily plotted from his letters. Of *Love and Mr. Lewisham* he wrote in 1900, "Be assured of my appreciation of your humour and your pathos—your homely truth and your unquenchable fancy. I am not sure that I see your *idea*—I mean your Subject, so to speak, as determined or constituted: but in short the thing is a bloody little chunk of life, of no small substance." *Kipps* in 1905 left James "prostrate with admiration," yet he thought the book "not so much a masterpiece as a mere born gem," a pearl brought up by a diver. In *The New Machiavelli* of 1911 James had only praise for Wells's "life and force and temperament, that fulness of endowment and easy impudence of genius." Yet Wells had totally disregarded *method*, with the result that the book could only be compared to "a far-flaring even though turbid and smoky lamp, projecting the most vivid and splendid golden splotches, *creating* them about the field—shining scattered innumerable morsels of a huge smashed mirror." After *Marriage* in 1912 James in effect abandoned hope for Wells. He wrote to Mrs. Humphry Ward: "Strange to me—in his affair—the co-existence of so much talent with so little art, so much life with (so to speak) so little living! But of him there is much to say, for I really think him more interesting by his faults than he will probably ever manage to be in any other way; and he is a most vivid and violent object-lesson."

III

So much life . . . so little living. It depended of course on what was meant by *life*. James was expressing again what he had expressed in other terms in *The Ambassadors*. Life was a jelly, quivering and formless, and it had to be poured into a mould, given shape and form, if the result was to be finished art instead of raw data. James was not alone during these years in urging upon Wells the need for discipline, for finding a characteristic form into which he could pour the extraordinary vitality of his mind. This is a principal theme of the quite different corre-spondence between Wells and Arnold Bennett, a novelist much closer than James to Wells's world. Bennett con-stantly denounced his friend's happy unconsciousness of his "artistic limitations," his invariable preference for "the work which costs the least trouble," his perverse dislike of the nineteenth-century French masters on whose books Bennett modelled his own fiction, and his insistence on "practising the higher literary carelessness" after "the example of most great English writers." Another of Wells's fellow-novelists took a different line. Joseph Conrad grew disturbed in contemplating the effect that Wells's sociological preoccupations and his zeal for reform might come to have on his fiction. He granted that the position of influence Wells had attained over the younger generation was an "enviable fate," yet he urged Wells in the future to make his art "contain his convictions, where they would be seen in a more perfect light. . . . When all the questions are settled, reopened and settled again the story of Mr. Lewisham's contact with Love will have an unchanged significance both as an artist's vision and as a life's record. It will never grow archaic or lose its meaning as a mere statement of view may appear to the greater enlightenment of our distant descendants." And when Conrad at length saw that Wells was incapable of following his advice, he broke with him, saying: "The difference between us, Wells, is fundamental. You don't care for humanity but think they are to be improved. I love humanity but know they are not!"

Desmond MacCarthy once observed that "Mr. Wells has always been set on believing that the value of a novel depends upon the amount of good stuff in it; that it is a

hold-all into which you can cram anything you have
ready. Had patience been added to his cluster of extraordinary gifts he would have been among the world's
great novelists." But as the years passed Wells grew
increasingly impatient; he took life on the run. After dis-
cussing the art of fiction with a dozen fellow-novelists,
he decided to give wider utterances to his minority view.
In May of 1911 he spoke on "The Scope of the Novel"
under the auspices of the Times Book Club. This talk,
the final title of which was "The Contemporary Novel,"
constituted a reply to James, to Conrad, to Bennett and
to other candid friends. Hitherto Wells had not tried to
make out a coherent case for his kind of fiction. He had
contented himself with occasional *boutades* such as his
reference in *Mankind in the Making* to "the artist who
lives angrily in his stuffy little corner of pure technique."
Now, however, he advanced two ideas: he argued that
there can be no prescriptive pattern for the novel and that
the novel is a means rather than an end in itself. The
novel had to be "kept free from the restrictions imposed
upon it by the fierce pedantries of those who would define
a general form for it." In England it was characteristic-
ally a "discursive thing; it is not a single interest, but a
woven tapestry of interests." He contended that the
underlying fallacy in much criticism of the novel was the
assumption that fiction, like story-telling, aims at a single,
concentrated impression.

In support of his contention that the novel could not be

an end in itself he pointed out that the world was witnessing "a great intellectual revolution." What should the novel be, then, if not the "social mediator, the vehicle of understanding, the instrument of self-examination, the parade of morals? . . . Before we have done, we will have all life within the scope of the novel." James had said as much a dozen years earlier in his essay on "The Future of the Novel." The crucial difference between the two statements was that James, in including all life within the scope of the novel, urged on this very account the need to give to this life a shaping form, that is, not to allow life to run away with the form.

From 1911 Wells took an almost perverse pleasure in boasting that he was a journalist and nothing more. He continued to send James his books, knowing that each volume would elicit still another formidable rejoinder on the craft of his fiction, but a note of persiflage began to creep into his answers. To James's elaborate dissection of *Marriage* he replied impenitently that his next book would be mere "mixed pickles." "I am, like so many poor ladies, determined to be worse before I am better . . . It is, I hope, a prolonged acute disease rather than a chronic decay, and thereafter I will seek earnestly to make my pen lead a decent life, pull myself together, and think of Form." And, in answering James's reproaches concerning *The Passionate Friends*, Wells became extravagantly depreciatory in James's own manner. "My art is abortion . . . The most finished [of my books] have still hare lips, cleft palates, open crania . . . I want to embrace your feet and bedew your knees with tears—of quite unfruitful penitence."

James could hardly have failed to read and to disagree with "The Scope of the Novel," which was published in the *Fortnightly Review* (November 1911) and the *Atlantic Monthly* (January 1912). Early in 1912 a further difference occurred, one which led to several long and close talks between the two at the Reform Club, where James usually stayed when he came up to London. Both had been elected members of the Academic Committee of the Royal Society of Literature. Wells refused to serve. James, with his strong professional sense and his continental acceptance of academies, argued that Wells would contribute much in the committee that would be helpful to the cause of letters. He saw in the body a hope for "continuity and coherency" in an age of declining literary standards. Wells pointed out that as early as *Mankind in the Making* he had opposed anything like an academy. The writer, he argued, was essentially "anarchic" and flourished best in an atmosphere of freedom and diversity. It is strange to reflect that Wells, who was prepared to make literature a vehicle for social ideas, should now have espoused spiritual anarchism for authors —strange until we realize that Wells was an anarchist in all that he did, an out-sailing adventurer who would make literature responsible only to his own soaring ideas and ambitions. James stood on the side of art and responsibility. Art was order and no artist could be "anarchic." In a letter to Edmund Gosse, James gave Wells the benefit of any doubt he might have entertained. "He has cut loose from literature clearly—practically altogether. This settles the matter . . . He *had* decently to decline, and I think it decent of him to have felt that." He added that Wells was "absolutely immovable" on the subject.

IV

It is improbable that H. G. Wells would have turned from the gentle raillery that is to be found in his private letters to cruel public mockery of Henry James if he had not received what he deemed to be substantial provocation. This occurred in 1914 when the American novelist published in *The Times Literary Supplement* a two-instalment article entitled "The Younger Generation." Later that year he expanded the article for inclusion in *Notes on Novelists*. It was an unusual performance for James, and in some ways his least responsible piece of criticism. He undertook to survey the young writers, to try to take the measure of a new generation. He wrote to Bruce Richmond of *The Times* that he wanted to treat "half a dozen *selectable* cases"—but the cases he finally ended up with included friends like Edith Wharton, whom he could hardly overlook, or young admirers like Hugh Walpole, whose writings he could praise only in ambiguous terms. To Conrad he could accord the recognition of a master who sees himself reflected in a disciple's mirror; and his heaviest salvo was reserved for H. G. Wells and Arnold Bennett, who became for him the arch-representatives of the over-loaded, formless novel, which failed alike in discipline and in economy. James began with the complaints that had earlier fathered his tales "The Figure in the Carpet" and "The Death of the Lion." Criticism had not yet learned, he said, how to deal with the novel as an art form. This was a condition of "responsibility declined in the face of disorder." His survey of the younger generation was designed to restore a little order: it included figures such as Gilbert Cannan, since lost from view, but nodded at, and looked away from, D. H. Lawrence, who had just published *Sons and Lovers*.

In Wells and Bennett, James saw writers who tried to avoid sentimentality by "saturation in the actual. "They squeeze out to the utmost the plump and more or less juicy orange of a particular acquainted state and let this affirmation of energy, however directed or undirected, constitute for them the 'treatment' of the theme." Though James does not disdain saturation, he thinks it only half of the novelist's authority, the other half being "the application he is inspired to make of that advantage." Only so can "the pleasure of appreciation" be realized. Tolstoy, James argued, was the "great illustrative master-hand on all this ground of disconnection of method from matter." And he repeated what he had said

c

both publicly and privately before: that the Russian writer should stand as "a caution" and only "execrably, pestilentially, as a model." The failure to *exhibit* and *present* is the most marked feature of his work; and Wells and Bennett, and their followers, derive from Tolstoy "by multiplied if diluted transmissions." Just as there is no "centre of interest or . . . sense of the whole" in *War and Peace*, so there is none in *The Old Wives' Tales* or *The Passionate Friends*. The reader is left with the simple amusement of watching the orange being squeezed.

Wells took this article, in which James's underlying severity was masked for superficial readers by his unvarying courtesy and moderation of statement, as an unfriendly act. The essay seemed to him an elaborate exercise in denigration, quite inconsistent with the praise that James had lavished on his books during the past fifteen years. What he overlooked was that this private praise had always been qualified by private criticism, which James was now publicly repeating in more generalized form. "The Younger Generation" was not really the act of treachery that Wells implied. But we can understand, nevertheless, how his anger was aroused by James's thrice repeated image for Bennett's fiction, "the squeezing of a plump and juicy orange." This brought to mind James's comparison of Bennett's *Hilda Lessways* two years earlier to "the slow wringing out of a dirty sponge." It confirmed Wells in his conviction that James was behaving disingenuously.

Wells was working at this time on the book eventually published as *Boon*, the most esoteric and chaotic of all his works. He had conceived it as early as 1901, written three chapters in 1905, and returned to it from time to time in the troubled period following the publication of *Ann Veronica* in 1909, when his name was anathema to a large part of the respectable British public. But it was not until the year of the First World War that he found in himself the animus necessary to carry the book to completion. *Boon* is a strange revelation of Wells's state of mind during the "phase of social acquiescence" in which he was working to establish himself as a writer. Throughout this period he had sought to play the London literary game according to the prevailing rules; but all the while his "outsider" eyes had seen its standards as imposed largely by the venal, the hypocritical, the incompetent, the feebly genteel. The exasperation that for twenty years had been mounting steadily within him—reinforcing the old exasperations of his impoverished boyhood—at last found its vent in *Boon*.

The book purports to be a selection from the private papers of a deceased writer named George Boon. His published works are impeccably conventional only because he was in the habit of dictating them to a Miss Bathwick, the perfect embodiment of middle-class respectability. She would interrupt him, or, if necessary, leave the room, whenever he veered into dangerous territory. To relieve his mind, however, Boon has composed a number of "secret writings," one of which, "The Mind of the Race," presents "a kind of Chatauqua conference of our literary world," patterned on Peacock's dialogue novels and Mallock's *New Republic*. Boon here "sets out with astonishing frankness just what he could let himself think about that literary world from which he derived his handsome income and fame." "If I offend, it is their fault!" Wells makes Boon say, ". . . My criticism is absolutely honest. Some of them are my dearest friends." To which his interlocutor of the moment replies: "They won't be . . . when all this appears." The friends and acquaintances included Belloc, Chesterton, Conrad, Hueffer, Gosse, Shaw, Hugh Walpole, and—as we shall see—Henry James.

As *Boon* stood in March 1914, James figured in it only once, paired decorously and innocuously with John Singer Sargent. But after the publication of the article on "The Younger Generation" Wells wrote an entirely new chapter entitled "Of Art, Of Literature, Of Mr. Henry James," which he inserted in his manuscript. Into this chapter he packed all the things about James and his work that had irritated him and amused him during the past seventeen years. He begins with a parody of James's elaborate and involved manner of speech as—to use Wells's image—James opens and bleeds slowly from one after another vein of thought in the warm bath of his sympathy. There follows a passage in which Wells's idea of literature is contrasted with

James's. He takes "The Younger Generation" as his starting point and develops his famous comparison of the Jamesian novel to "a church lit but without a congregation to distract you, with every light and line focused on the high altar. And on the altar, very reverently placed, intensely there, is a dead kitten, an egg-shell, a bit of string." Finally the plot of a Jamesian novel on the pattern of "The Turn of the Screw" or "Covering End" is briefly sketched. It is titled *The Spoils of Mr. Blandish*. The central figure is both in appearance and character "the very soul of Henry James," as Wells had come to envision him. We learn how Mr. Blandish leases Samphire House, which he regards with all the reverence James entertained for Lamb House; how he finds the ideal butler with "the perfect name—Mutimer"; how the house appears to be haunted by the ghosts of past inhabitants; how obscure but complicated inquiries are set in motion by a typically Jamesian group of characters to discover the secret of Samphire House; and how the mystery is resolved in a farcical and utterly un-Jamesian finale.

When *Boon* was published, Wells had the audacity—or a total failure in empathy—to leave a copy for James at his club. The letter which James wrote in acknowledgment is a classic of the epistolary art. Even under this sharp provocation, his response was controlled and dignified. He expressed his profound regret that *Boon* must terminate his friendship with Wells. Its publication

represented "the collapse of a bridge which made com-
munication possible." His discovery that Wells regarded
him as an "unmitigated mistake"—he was careful to
make clear—did not shake his loyalty to the standards
that he had upheld all his life. Wells's conciliatory
response evoked an eloquent final defence by James of
his conception of life and art. And so the association of
the two men ended.

V

Henry James died less than a year after, in 1916. But
the chapter on him in *Boon* returned to haunt Wells
again and again in later life. Preoccupied as he was with
his self-imposed task of educating England and the
world, the defences he offered at odd moments for conduct that, after all, was difficult to defend, were curious
and contradictory. We shall cite only the most wildly
illogical of all, which has a particular interest to-day for
the unexpected terms in which it refers to two respected
writers who still adorn the literary world—and for its
anticipation forty years ago of what is sometimes fondly
regarded as the wholly modern concept of posthumous
guilt by association. Wells is writing in 1916 to Hugh
Walpole, with whom he had just compounded a quarrel
originating in *Boon*:

I think the fuss a lot of you made about the James
parody in *Boon* was a little unjust. The old man was a
little treacherous to me in a very natural sort of way and

the James cult has been overdone. Anyhow nothing I've ever written or said or anyone has ever written or said about James can balance the extravagant dirtiness of [Percy] Lubbock and his friends in boycotting Rebecca West's book on him in *The Times Literary Supplement*. My blood still boils at the thought of those pretentious academic greasers conspiring to down a friendless girl (who can write any of them out of sight) in the name of loyalty to literature.

The abiding importance of the documents in which the troubled relationship of the two famous novelists is recorded lies in the illumination they provide of the aesthetic of the novel; they illuminate on the one hand the artist who is devoted wholly to fathoming and re-creating human experience, and on the other the writer unconcerned with aesthetic matters for whom literature is merely one way of communicating and advancing his ideas. The novel was, for Wells, a convenience, something to be used for specific ends; for James the novel was the most characteristic art-form of our time, intricate and human, to be practised with professional skill and all the resources of the artist's imagination. Wells's mockery of James both in *Boon* and in his "Digression About Novels" is more than a failure in perception; it reveals that this remarkable man, whose imagination could soar through space and time and create tales of wonderful new worlds, was yet limited and earth-bound when it came to understanding the true nature of art. Thus Wells in the end became an irritant, a provoking force, which drew from James the admirable—and, as it happened, the final—statement of his credo embodied in his letter terminating their friendship. A few years earlier he had had occasion to make a similar statement to Bernard Shaw, who had written to him: "People don't want works of art from you: they want help: they want above all encouragement." James had then replied that if Shaw held such views and "if we didn't both *like* to talk—there would be scarce use in our talking at all." Works of art, he went on to say, "are capable of saying more things to a man about himself than any other 'works' whatever are capable of doing—and it's only by thus saying as much to him as possible, by saying, as nearly as we can, all there is, and in as many ways and on as many sides, and with a vividness of presentation, that 'art,' and art alone, is an adequate mistress of, that we enable him to pick and choose and compare and know, enable him to arrive at any sort of synthesis that isn't, through all its superficialities and vacancies, a base and illusive humbug."

But now his statement rose to a higher eloquence in answering Wells's challenge. And though Wells was to survive James for three decades and to offer several versions of their famous dispute, the final word remains with the old master of Rye and Chelsea:

I *have* no view of life and literature, I maintain, other than that our form of the latter in especial is admirable exactly by its range and variety, its plasticity and liberality, its fairly living on the sincere and shifting experience of the individual practitioner. That is why I have always so admired your so free and strong application of it, the particular rich receptacle of intelligences and impressions emptied out with an energy of its own, that your genius constitutes; and *that* is in particular why . . . I pronounced it curious and interesting that you should find the case I constitute myself only ridiculous and vacuous to the extent of your having to proclaim your sense of it.

And so on to the summing up, that art "*makes* life, makes interest, makes importance" and that there is no substitute for the beauty and the force of the process. In writing this letter James had turned his other cheek, and in a manner that Wells could never answer nor forget.

I

H. G. WELLS

An Evening at The Play [1]

I BEGAN the New Year [1895] with my first and only regular job on a London daily. Cust [2] had promised that I should have the next vacancy, whatever it was, on the *Pall Mall*, and the lot fell upon the dramatic criticism. I was summoned by telegram. "Here," said Cust and thrust two small pieces of coloured paper into my hand.

"What are these?" I asked.

"Theatres. Go and do 'em."

"Yes," I said and reflected. "I'm willing to have a shot at it, but I ought to warn you that so far, not counting the Crystal Palace Pantomime and Gilbert and Sullivan, I've been only twice to a theatre."

"Exactly what I want," said Cust. "You won't be in the gang. You'll make a break."

"One wears evening dress?"

It was not in Cust's code of manners to betray astonishment. "Oh yes. To-morrow night especially. The Haymarket."

We regarded each other thoughtfully for a moment.

---

[1] *Experiment in Autobiography* (London, 1934), pp. 534–537.
[2] Harry Cust, editor of the *Pall Mall Gazette*.

"Right oh," said I and hurried round to a tailor named Millar in Charles Street who knew me to be solvent. "Can you make me evening clothes by to-morrow night?" I asked, "Or must I hire them?"

The clothes were made in time but in the foyer I met Cust and George Steevens ready to supply a criticism if I failed them and nothing came to hand from me. But I did the job in a fashion and posted my copy fairly written out in its bright red envelope before two o'clock in the morning in the Mornington Road pillar box. The play was "*An Ideal Husband*, a new and original play of modern life by Oscar Wilde."

That was on the third of January 1895, and all went well. On the fifth I had to do *Guy Domville*, a play by Henry James at the St. James's Theatre. This was a more memorable experience. It was an extremely weak drama. James was a strange unnatural human being, a sensitive man lost in an immensely abundant brain, which had had neither a scientific nor a philosophical training, but which was by education and natural aptitude alike, formal, formally aesthetic, conscientiously fastidious and delicate. Wrapped about in elaborations of gesture and speech, James regarded his fellow creatures with a face of distress and a remote effort at intercourse, like some victim of enchantment placed in the centre of an immense bladder. His life was unbelievably correct and his home at Rye one of the most perfect pieces of suitably furnished Georgian architecture imaginable. He was an unspotted bachelor.

He had always been well off and devoted to artistic ambitions; he had experienced no tragedy and he shunned the hoarse laughter of comedy; and yet he was consumed by a gnawing hunger for dramatic success. In this performance he had his first and last actual encounter with the theatre.[1]

Guy Domville was one of those rare ripe exquisite Catholic Englishmen of ancient family conceivable only by an American mind, who gave up the woman he loved to an altogether coarser cousin, because his religious vocation was stronger than his passion. I forget the details of the action. There was a drinking scene in which Guy and the cousin, for some obscure purpose of discovery, pretended to drink and, instead, poured their wine furtively into a convenient bowl of flowers upon the table between them. Guy was played by George Alexander, at first in a mood of refined solemnity and then as the intimations of gathering disapproval from pit and gallery increased, with stiffening desperation. Alexander at the close had an incredibly awkward exit. He had to stand at a door in the middle of the stage, say slowly "Be keynd to Her. . . . *Be* keynd to Her" and depart. By nature Alexander had a long face, but at that moment with audible defeat before him, he seemed the longest and dismallest face, all face, that I have ever seen. The

---

[1] James had one play, *The American*, produced before *Guy Domville*, and another, *The High Bid*, more than a decade after. An account of these productions is to be found in *The Complete Plays of Henry James* (ed. Edel), 1949.

slowly closing door reduced him to a strip, to a line, of perpendicular gloom. The uproar burst like a thunderstorm as the door closed and the stalls responded with feeble applause. Then the tumult was mysteriously allayed. There were some minutes of uneasy apprehension. "Author" cried voices. "Au-thor!" The stalls, not understanding, redoubled their clapping.

Disaster was too much for Alexander that night. A spasm of hate for the writer of those fatal lines must surely have seized him. With incredible cruelty he led the doomed James, still not understanding clearly how things were with him, to the middle of the stage, and there the pit and gallery had him. James bowed; he knew it was the proper thing to bow. Perhaps he had selected a few words to say, but if so they went unsaid. I have never heard any sound more devastating than the crescendo of booing that ensued. The gentle applause of the stalls was altogether overwhelmed. For a moment or so James faced the storm, his round face white, his mouth opening and shutting and then Alexander, I hope in a contrite mood, snatched him back into the wings.

That was my first sight of Henry James with whom I was later to have a sincere yet troubled friendship. We were by nature and training profoundly unsympathetic. He was the most consciously and elaborately artistic and refined human being I ever encountered, and I swam in the common thought and feeling of my period, with an irregular abundance of rude knowledge, aggressive judgments and a disposition to get to close quarters with Madame Fact even if it meant a scuffle with her. James never scuffled with Fact; he treated her as a perfect and unchallengable lady; he never questioned a single stitch or flounce of the conventions and interpretations in which she presented herself. He thought that for every social occasion a correct costume could be prescribed and a correct behaviour defined. On the table (an excellent piece) in his hall at Rye lay a number of caps and hats, each with its appropriate gloves and sticks, a tweed cap and a stout stick for the Marsh, a soft comfortable deer-stalker if he were to turn aside to the Golf Club, a light-brown felt hat and a cane for a morning walk down to the Harbour, a grey felt with a black band and a gold-headed cane of greater importance, if afternoon calling in the town was afoot. He retired at set times to a charming room in his beautiful walled garden and there he worked, dictating with a slow but not unhappy circum-spection, the novels that were to establish his position in the world of discriminating readers. They are novels from which all the fiercer experiences are excluded; even their passions are so polite that one feels that they were gratified, even at their utmost intimacy, by a few seemly gestures; and yet the stories are woven with a peculiar humorous, faintly fussy, delicacy, that gives them a flavour like nothing else in the language. When you want to read and find reality too real, and hard story-telling tiresome, you may find Henry James good company. For generations to come a select type of reader will brighten appreciatively to *The Spoils of Poynton*, *The Ambassadors*, *The Tragic Muse*, *The Golden Bowl* and many of the stories.

2

H. G. WELLS

"Guy Domville" at the St. James's [1]

MR. HENRY JAMES has selected for his theme an excursion into the world, a "voyage of discovery" for three brief months, taken by a young man trained as a priest, and for his period the picturesque days immediately preceding the French Revolution. Guy Domville, private tutor to the son of the young and beautiful widow, Mrs. Peverel, is preparing to leave that position to enter the Roman Catholic Church, when an unexpected hunting accident terminates the elder branch of the family and makes him the "last of the Domvilles." The first intimation of this is brought to him at Mrs. Peverel's house by that elderly and impoverished nobleman, Lord Devenish. This Lord Devenish is the Mephistopheles of the excursion; he appeals to Guy's family pride, to his youthful love of life, and skilfully induces Mrs. Peverel to help in dissuading Guy from the cloister. Mrs. Peverel loves Guy and Guy loves Mrs. Peverel, but having been requested in the

[1] *Pall Mall Gazette*, 7 January 1895.

Miles Standish fashion to undertake the case of Frank Humber, he apparently considers himself in honour bound to forego her. He accompanies Lord Devenish to London, sees life, and appears in the second act sadly changed, no longer an earthly saint, but a very brilliant and accomplished gentleman in scarlet and steel. He gambles and drinks freely, and is about to be married, quite against her will, to Mary Brasier, the reputed daughter of a cousin by marriage. Really, however, Mary is the child of an intrigue between Lord Devenish and Mrs. Domville, her mother. George Round (Lieutenant R.N.), the courier and accepted lover of Mary, returns on the morning of the marriage. He moors his boat at the back of Mrs. Domville's house—it is at Richmond— early in the second act, and comes and goes with great freedom and pertinacity through the conservatory. Then follows a remarkable scene: Round pretends to be drunk and tries to make Guy Domville really so; Domville perceives his intention, pours away the wine into a bowl of flowers, and also pretends to be drunk. His pretence successfully deceives Round, but not Mary. However, after numerous exits and entrances it ends happily in Domville understanding how matters lie, and Round retires to his boat for the last time through Domville's apartments, with Mary, presumably to fly to Twickenham and marry. Therewith Domville leaves London in a fit of disgust, and returns to the pining Mrs. Peverel. This second act is the weak part of the play. It is tedious and

D

impossible; people come and go in the house unchallenged, like rabbits in a warren, and it was played with a singular lack of spirit. Moreover, as it was acted there was scarcely a hint of Guy's growing disgust with life, especially of such life as Lord Devenish typifies, a disgust that forms the key to the third act.

Lord Devenish, after the collapse of his marriage scheme, for no earthly reason, hurries off to Mrs. Peverel to tell her of the business. Guy arrives while he is there, and the nobleman, being anxious to escape him, is hustled off into another room. Guy is proposing marriage to Mrs. Peverel, when he discovers the glove of Lord Devenish on the table. It is the taint of the world, and in a passionate revulsion he resolves to proceed to his monastery, commending Frank Humber to Mrs. Peverel in his last farewell.

It is [a] fine conception, but altogether too weakly developed. The circumstances of Guy's disillusionment are quite inadequate, and that and the complexity of the second act are the faults of Mr. James. But the play fails chiefly through the imperfect appreciation of the players. A less convincing performance than that of Mr. Elliot as the subtle and scheming Lord Devenish it would be hard to imagine. He is made up in a mode of caricature, and presents the extreme of fashionable folly—he might have come out of Hogarth, but he has certainly no business to come into this play. In the first act Mr. Alexander, as Guy Domville, is a didactic puritan; in the second a

fine generous blade; in the third he is that impossible,
noble, iron-grey Mr. Alexander that we have seen before. Then it was Mrs. Saker's business to be a woman of
fifty—a duty she has neglected; and she wears a costume
that may possibly be historically correct, but which was
incredible to half the audience, and which touches the
note of caricature at absolutely the wrong moment. To
the rest of the cast, however, no objection can be raised.
They did their work decently and in order.

The play was received with marked disapproval by a
considerable section of the audience. Yet it was, save for
the defects we have pointed out, a play finely conceived
and beautifully written. But the entire workmanship was
too delicate for acting; and whether that is the fault of
player or playwright is a very pretty question. A play
written for the stage may very well be compared to a
pen-and-ink drawing that is to undergo reproduction by
some cheap photographic process. Delicate turns, soft
shades, refinements of grey *must* be avoided; bold strokes,
black and firm—that is all that is possible. The thing is
to be reproduced on such a scale as to carry across un-
impaired to the pit and gallery. Delicate work simply
blurs and looks weak. The better the process, of course,
the finer the work it will render; with such acting as one
may dream of, this play might still have been a very
beautiful one in spite of its structural defect. But as it was,
it is undeniable that the delicacy of the play degenerated
into a hectic weakness; and of all defects feebleness is the

one most abhorred of the gods. The diagnosis points to an early deathbed; only a tonic treatment and the utmost gentleness on the part of those concerned in it can save the life of the play. Mr. Elliot in particular must moderate his grimaces, and Mrs. Saker must be toned down. And for the tonic treatment—that is for Mr. James and Mr. Alexander to consider. As it stands at present, the second act is hopeless, and the mental evolution of Guy Domville altogether incredible.

3

JAMES TO WELLS[1]

Lamb House, Rye.
Saturday [1898]

DEAR MR. WELLS.

Your letter covers me with shame and confusion—in addition to filling me with interest and sympathy. I

[1] Although undated and fragmentary, this letter and the next are the first James wrote to Wells, during the period when Wells was moving into Beach Cottage at Sandgate while recovering from a prolonged kidney ailment. In his *Experiment in Autobiography* Wells describes what must have been James's first visit to him at New Romney, just before he moved to Beach Cottage. James arrived on a bicycle with his fellow-cyclist, Edmund Gosse. They had come from Rye, where James lived in Lamb House, a short distance away. Years later Wells discovered that the motive for their visit, never explicitly avowed, was to ascertain on behalf of the Royal Literary Fund whether the ailing Wells required financial assistance.

should have been over to see you before this were it not
that my little house has been stuffed with people and my
attention wrenched—even from hideously belated work
—to the supplying of their strikingly numerous wants.
I shall be more free next week, and on one of the earliest
possible days of it I will knock at your door. I shall not
be satisfied that a house is inaccessible to you in this
place until I have threshed the matter out with you, and
with Mr. Smith here—and the householders in general.
This is a little place so amiable as to be worth—as will
doubtless have occurred to you—some sacrifice and
effort. Alas, as I read over your sad story of your so
intimately personal wrongs, I feel that you are already
but too familiar with those rapacious divinities ... [. . .] [1]
you to have written me so explicitly, and also to know
anything at all about my recent small fiction—the most
insignificant of literary accidents.[2] Again please believe,
till I can better it by a handshake, in the very active participation of yours, and Mrs. Wells's, [. . .] [3]

P.S. I *think* she went without !

[1] About six words cut away.
[2] Probably "The Turn of the Screw". [3] Signature cut away.

4

JAMES TO WELLS

Lamb House, Rye.
Tuesday p.m. [1898]

[DEAR] H. G. WELLS,

Forgive my delay (the result of the stranger—in too great abundance—within my gates: pressure on pressure,) to participate thus articulately in your weal and your woe. I wish there had been less woe—the woe sounds awful: but it's something to have an address, and Beach Cottage, though a trifle gritty, suggests views—and views may suggest something else. I groan, however, to think what you must have [. . .] and how despair [. . .] by your couch [. . .][1] to catch, the first thing in the a.m., your early waking eye. Thank God, at any rate, now, that you are, if not housed, at least cottaged. I shall take the earliest opportunity of following up the conducting scent you mention. I hope, through it all, your convalescence bravely maintains itself. I was at Romney on Sunday, and it looked empty and anxious. It was most good of you to write to me. I do mean to reach you; and I send all sympathy to Mrs. Wells. Believe me yours ve[ry . . .][2]

[1] A word or two has been cut away in this and the two preceding hiatuses.

[2] Signature cut away.

5

JAMES TO WELLS

Lamb House, Rye.
Dec. 9th, 1898.

MY DEAR H. G. WELLS,

Your so liberal and graceful letter is to my head like coals of fire—so repeatedly for all these weeks have I had feebly to suffer frustrations in the matter of trundling over the marsh to ask for your news and wish for your continued amendment. The shortening days and the deepening mud have been at the bottom of this affair. I never get out of the house till 3 o'clock, when night is quickly at one's heels. I would have taken a regular day—I mean started in the a.m.—but have been so ridden, myself, by the black care of an unfinished and *running* (galloping, leaping and bounding,) serial[1] that parting with a day has been like parting with a pound of flesh. I am still a neck ahead, however, and *this* week will see me through: I accordingly hope very much to be able to turn up on one of the ensuing days. I will sound a horn, so that you yourself be not absent on the chase. Then I will express more articulately my appreciation of your various signs of critical interest, as well as assure you of my sympathy in your own martyrdom. What will you

[1] Serialisation of *The Awkward Age* had begun on 1 October 1898 in *Harper's Weekly*.

have? It's all a grind and a bloody battle—as well as a considerable lark, and the difficulty itself is the refuge from the vulgarity. Bless your heart, I think I could easily say worse of the T[*urn*] of the s[*crew*], the young woman, the spooks, the style, the everything, than the worst any one else could manage. One knows the *most* damning things about one's self. Of course I had, about my young woman, to take a very sharp line. The grotesque business I had to make her picture and the childish psychology I had to make her trace and present, were, for me at least, a very difficult job, in which absolute lucidity and logic, a singleness of effect, were imperative. Therefore I had to rule out subjective complications of her own—play of tone etc.; and keep her impersonal save for the most obvious and indispensable little note of neatness, firmness and courage—without which she wouldn't have had her data.[1] But the thing is essentially a pot-boiler and a *jeu d'esprit.*

[1] Many critics have cited this passage as refutation of the thesis that the ghosts in "The Turn of the Screw" were imagined by the governess. James actually is explaining to Wells how he kept the governess "impersonal"—so that she is not even named. In his later preface to the ghostly tale he may have been alluding to Wells's inquiries when he wrote: "I recall . . . a reproach made me by a reader capable evidently, for the time, of some attention, but not quite capable of enough, who complained that I hadn't sufficiently 'characterised' my young woman engaged in her labyrinth; hadn't endowed her with signs and marks, features and humours, hadn't in a word invited her to deal with her own mystery as well as with that of Peter Quint, Miss Jessel and the hapless children." To which James added: "We have surely as much of her own nature as we can swallow in watching it reflect her anxieties and inductions." He

With the little play,[1] the absolute creature of its conditions, I had simply to make up a deficit and take a small *revanche*. For three mortal years had the actress[2] for whom it was written (utterly to try to *fit*) persistently failed to produce it, and I couldn't wholly waste my labour. The B[ritish] P[ublic] won't read a play with the mere names of the speakers—so I simply paraphrased these and added such indications as might be the equivalent of decent acting—a history and an evolution that seem to me moreover explicatively and sufficiently smeared all over the thing. The moral is of course Don't write one-act plays.

But I didn't mean thus to sprawl. I envy your hand your needle-pointed fingers. As you don't say that you're *not* better I prepare myself to be greatly struck with the same, and send kind regards to your wife.

Believe me yours ever,

HENRY JAMES

P.S. What's this about something in some newspaper?—I read least of all—from long and deep experience—what my friends write about me, and haven't read the things you mention. I suppose it's because they know I don't that they dare!

---

further remarks in his preface, in this same context, that it had been a question of "our young woman's keeping crystalline her record of so many intense anomalies and obscurities—by which I don't of course mean her explanation of them, a different matter."

[1] "Covering End," which with "The Turn of the Screw" makes up the volume entitled *The Two Magics*. 　　[2] Ellen Terry.

6

WELLS TO JAMES

Beach Cottage
Granville Road
Sandgate.
[*Jan.* 16, 1899]

DEAR HENRY JAMES.

I have continued to think about the *Two Magics*—the *Turn of the Screw*, I mean—and latterly with an increasing discomfort. Novel and disagreeable as the conviction is, I think now that the other alternative is right. The story is not wrong—I was. My conversion was accompanied by the profound conviction of sin and culminated in the small hours. I came to Grace in this way. On the assumption that this story is wrong, it should be possible for the 'prentice even to indicate the right way. I had one or two walks and several hours by the fire, and a night (some time before the night of Grace) pursuing the obvious remedy into blind alleys (where it vanished). Then it was resolved that the story was impossible and some convention had to be arranged. What was the minimum convention possible? And so, to enlightenment.

I've had a profitable time and I shan't make such comments on your work again. It isn't at all a lovely story but

I treated it with a singularly vulgar lack of respect, and
if you were not a novelist I should doubt of your for-
giveness.

We have both been ill and our servant too and as one
of us has to be about at least it has been a sort of Puss-in-
the-Corner game, but we are getting better now.

Our garden plot has been demolished by the sea and
the neighbours have been driven from their homes by sea
water and shingle, with which God in his wisdom has
seen fit to swamp their homes. He has also made a fresh
breach in Sandgate Castle, and much mischief eastward.

Yours very faithfully

H. G. WELLS

7

JAMES TO WELLS

Lamb House, Rye.

Sunday p.m.

[Nov. 12, 1899]

MY DEAR WELLS.

This is a word to thank you for your liberal response
to my poor letter and for your friendly hospitality of
attitude: even though, by a peculiar perversity, I shall
not be able to signal across to you for a week or two: "I
come *now*—I've started!" I'm obliged to go up to town,
very positively and inexorably, on Thursday or Friday,

(to see to the proper condition of my London flat,[1] which I have, thank God, let, furnished for a year;) and till then my time is rigidly mortgaged. I shall have to be 4 or 5 days in town; perhaps more; but as soon as I get back here I shall give you news of my approach. It won't— it can't, alas—be, for a reason that I will tell you, by bicycle; but it will be none the less prompt and direct for that. If the superstition of reaching you by that contrivance hadn't ridden me too much hitherto, I should have less ridiculously delayed.[2] I am much interested in what you tell me of your lying for a while at your length and desiring in that Olympian attitude to converse. You have a bed of laurels—and eke of banknotes, to recline on; but go to;—I also, *without* the mattress, will be Olympian; I will lie at *my* length—or breadth—beside you. This time it is not a case of my otherwise lying, and I will announce myself for an early day.

> Yours, and Mrs. Wells's, most truly
>
> HENRY JAMES

[1] James's flat was at 34 De Vere Gardens in Kensington. He had settled in 1898 in Lamb House, Rye, taking a long lease and later acquiring the property. He continued to sublet his flat and later gave it up, moving all its furnishings and his library to Rye. When in London he stayed at the Reform Club of which he had been a member since 1878.

[2] James's "superstition" was perhaps a tribute to Wells's enthusiasm for cycling, about the humours and pleasures of which he had written *The Wheels of Chance* in 1896.

8

JAMES TO WELLS

Lamb House, Rye.
November 20th, 1899.

MY DEAR H. G. WELLS,

You reduce me to mere gelatinous grovel. And the worst of it is that you know so well how. You, with a magnanimity already so marked as to be dazzling, sent me last summer a beautiful and discouraging volume [1] which I never mustered the right combination of minutes and terms to thank you for as it deserved—and then, perfectly aware that this shameful consciousness had practically converted me to quivering pulp, you let fly the shaft that has finished me in the fashion to which I now so distressfully testify. It is really most kind and charming of you, and the incident will figure largely in all your eventual biographies: yet it is almost more than I can bear. Seriously, I am extremely touched by your great humanity in the face of my atrocious bad manners. I think the reason *why* I didn't write to thank you for the magnificent romance of three or four months ago was that I simply dreaded a new occasion for still more purple perjury on the subject of coming over to see you! I *was*—I AM!— coming: and yet I couldn't—and I *can't!*—say it without

[1] *When the Sleeper Wakes* published in May 1899.

steeping myself afresh in apparent falsehood, to the eyes.
It is a weird tale of the *acharnement* of fate against an
innocent victim—I mean the history of my now immemorial failure: which I must not attempt to tell you
thus and now, but reserve for your convinced (from the
moment it isn't averted) ear on the day, and at the very
hour and moment, that failure is converted to victory. I
AM coming. I was lately extremely sorry to hear that you
have been somewhat unwell again—unless it be a gross
exaggeration. Heaven send that same. I AM coming. I
thank you very cordially for the 2 beautiful books. These
new tales [1] I have already absorbed and, to the best of my
powers, assimilated. You fill me with wonder and admiration. I think you have too great an unawareness of
difficulty—and (for instance) that the 4 big towns and
nice blue foods and belching news-trumpets etc., will
be the *least* of the differences in the days to come. . . .
But it's unfair to say that without saying a deal more:
which I can't, and [which] isn't worth it—and is besides
irrelevant and ungracious. Your spirit is huge, your
fascination irresistible, your resources infinite. *That* is
much more to the point. And I AM coming. I heartily
hope that if you *have* been incommoded it is already over,
and for a corrigible cause. I AM coming. Recall me,
please, kindly to Mrs. Wells, and believe me (I AM coming,) very truly (AND veraciously) yours

                                        HENRY JAMES

[1] *Tales of Space and Time*, published in November 1899.

9

JAMES TO WELLS

Lamb House, Rye.
January 29th 1900

MY DEAR WELLS.

It was very graceful of you to send me your book—I mean the particular masterpiece entitled *The Time Machine*,[1] after I had so *un*gracefully sought it at your hands. My proper punishment would have been promptly to have to pay for it—and this atonement I should certainly, for my indiscretion, already have made, had this muddy village facilitated the transaction by placing a bookseller's shop, or stand, in my path. (No Time Machine, as it happens, would suffice to measure the abysmal ages required by the local stationer to get a volume, as he calls it, down. Several, artlessly ordered by me, have been on their way down for months.) So I have had, as the next best thing, to bow my head to the extremity of simply reading you. You are very magnificent. I am beastly critical—but you are in a still higher degree wonderful. I re-write you, much, as I read—which is the highest tribute my damned impertinence can pay an author. I shall now not rest content till I have made up several other deficiencies—grossly

---

[1] Published in 1895.

accidental—in my perfect acquaintance with you. (Stay your hand—the aids to that extension are precisely the volumes on their way down. You *shall* cost me something—if it takes all my future—and all your own past.) So I am very particularly and knowingly grateful. I hope you and Mrs. Wells have kept warmer and drier and brighter and braver than I have done since my last parting with you. The weather, the news,[1] the solitary stress of January, Rye and the newspapers combined, have darkened my days and bedevilled my nights. I have felt like your Time Traveller at the bottom of his shaft. However, I suppose we all feel much alike—and shall have still more reason to yet. I hope poor Bob Stevenson[2] is resisting successfully his remedial agencies. If he does *that* there will indeed be hope for him. I think of him with pangs and pains and pities and send him my tender remembrance. Good night and all good wishes. With kind remembrances to your wife, yours most truly

HENRY JAMES

[1] The Boer War, with its initial succession of disasters for the English forces, had begun on 12 October 1899.

[2] R. A. M. Stevenson, cousin of Robert Louis Stevenson—the "Spring-Heeled Jack" of "Talk and Talkers"—had come to a Sandgate lodging to recuperate after a stroke. Wells, who had known him before his illness, later provided an impression of "his style of imaginative talking" in Ewart's account of a City of Women in *Tono-Bungay*.

10

JAMES TO WELLS

Lamb House, Rye.
Feb: 25 : 1900.

MY DEAR WELLS.

Ever since receiving your last note—or rather (excuse me,) so liberal letter, I've been moved to ask you if you couldn't feel free, some day before long (now that the light a little lingers,) to help me to answer it *viva voce* by coming over here for a night—which would be so much better than my merely trying to scrawl at you responsively and illegibly thus. I should be very glad indeed to see you, and could put you up not discomfortably—and if you had to get off the morrow a.m. the 9.38 hence would conveniently do it for you. You would find me alone, but the pleasure for me would be the less divided and defeated. *Then* we could talk! Think of it, dissolute man! The 1 (about) from Ashford will bring you in time for lunch, with my daily job by that time quite polished off. Name your day—almost any one would suit *me*; and do come. Commend me kindly to Mrs. Wells and believe me yours ever

HENRY JAMES

E

I I

JAMES TO WELLS

Lamb House, Rye

[1900?]

MY DEAR WELLS,

How well I understand and how much I commiserate!

My prayers are with you, even as your curses must be with your botherer.

But Wednesday 6th will do beautifully—no day better. I shall look for you therefore at this station by the arriving 1.29; and be there to guide your steps and (I trust) breathe my congratulations without an effect of derision.

Yours always, in haste

Thursday   HENRY JAMES

I 2

JAMES TO WELLS

Lamb House, Rye.

June 17th 1900.

MY DEAR WELLS.

I must delay no longer to thank you for the generous present of your new book [1]—which I wished to read

[1] *Love and Mr. Lewisham.*

before I broke silence. I now *have* read it, and can speak with assurance. I have found in it a great charm and a great deal of the real thing—that is of the note of life, if not *all* of it (as distinguished from the said great deal.) Why I haven't found "all" I will some day try and tell you: it may be more feasible viva voce. Meanwhile be assured of my appreciation of your humour and your pathos—your homely truth and your unquenchable fancy. I am not quite sure that I see your *idea*—I mean your Subject, so to speak, as determined or constituted: but in short the thing is a bloody little chunk of life, of no small substance, and I wish it a great and continuous fortune.—You will have felt, as I have done, the miserable sadness of poor Crane's so precipitated and, somehow, so unnecessary extinction.[1] I was at Brede Place this afternoon—and it looked conscious and cruel. My very kind regards to your wife. Yours, my dear Wells, most cordially

HENRY JAMES

[1] Stephen Crane had died a few days earlier in Germany of tuberculosis. For a while he and his wife had been neighbours of James's at Brede Place, and James had taken a personal interest in the welfare of his compatriot. Wells gives a vivid picture of life at Brede Place and of his friendship with the Cranes in *Experiment in Autobiography.*

13

JAMES TO WELLS

Lamb House, Rye.
December 9th 1900.

MY DEAR WELLS.

Your beautiful little sign-manual announces a fact on which I lose no time in congratulating you. I am delighted to think of you so handsomely and bravely encased as—by the prospectus you some time ago showed me (I vividly remember it,)—the world will now know you.[1] It's a grand showing, and you must be, and your wife, to whom my felicitations are still more marked, must be, in the first exquisite stages of amusement and exaltation. There are (I say it as a country gentleman of slightly longer standing,) stages *more* exquisite, shades of sensation—depth within depth, wheel within wheel, to come; but nothing really so ingenuous as the first delirium of occupation. How, by the way, it must have flashed up—a mere *thought* of a mountain road but the other day, and now an organic full-blown British home! I hope it hasn't—to meet a date, or anything of that sort—been shorn of any charm or curtailed of any joy. Long, at any rate, may your years be in it, and well-fitting your roof!

---

[1] Wells had recently moved into Spade House, Sandgate, which had been built for him by C. F. A. Voysey, a pioneer of architectural modernism. See *Experiment in Autobiography*, VII, 6.

I owe you still—I've owed you these many weeks, acknowledgment of a most kind letter sent me on the occasion of—having read my last book.[1] I seem to describe it as a copy of verses—and it was indeed more beautiful than much contemporary verse. It gave me extreme pleasure, but I acted in the spirit of a friend of mine who asserts that those who *answer answers* should be killed—and your letter was, in its grand way, an answer. The real response to it is something I'm toiling at now month after month [2]—in an anguish of not arrested but torturingly *un*arrested development. I am letting myself go—or letting the car of Juggernaut come freely, to boil down still more freely afterward. But it's a process of ruinous expense, and the parts I shall have to sacrifice are more finished than those I shall contrive to keep. It's not an inviolable irreducible whole, like your Domestic Idea. However, such as it is, I shall some day shovel it at your feet. And Spade House will properly contain the instrument for removing it in instalments. I go up to London on Monday for a longish stay; but after a while, in more genial conditions, I shall come over and toy with your knocker. I hope you are well in spite of everything and am with kind regards to your wife, yours, my dear Wells, most truly

HENRY JAMES

[1] *The Sacred Fount.*
[2] He had begun writing *The Ambassadors.*

14

JAMES TO WELLS

Lamb House, Rye.
April 30th 1901.

MY DEAR WELLS.

Your letter is most kind as well as most dainty—but the case is *this*: viz: that I *can't*, to my great sorrow, leave home even for a night before I've finished a most interminable task—the non-completion of which now rides me like a nightmare. I've a terrible belated Book [1] to get off my hands before I can indulge in *any* custom of exercise or sociability; and my predicament is so dire, my absence of margin so utter, and my desolation, generally, so grim, that every hour and every instant have their weight in the tragic scale. As soon as the burden *is* off my back—and the end, thank God, is in sight—I will come over with joy for the 2 nights you so hospitably suggest. I greatly want to see your house and all that is yours. I would venture to propose (as I hear from Conrad that he presently comes to Winchelsea for a certain time,[2]) that you put in, meanwhile, the 2 nights *here*; were it not that I have with me for the present my

[1] *The Ambassadors.*
[2] Conrad shortly afterwards settled at The Bungalow, Winchelsea.

brother and his wife and daughter [1]—which exhausts my house-room. Patience, therefore, a little—and things will be better. The House of the Spade will, I feel sure, find dug for itself a deeper seat in my desire by the time I am momentarily free. (For I've a few moments to change horses, simply, then: I must *immediately* thereafter take to the road again.) I send a very kind remembrance to your wife and am yours as faithfully as breathlessly, ever

HENRY JAMES

15

JAMES TO WELLS

Lamb House, Rye.

June 13*th* 1901

MY DEAR WELLS.

This is genial news—save that I am very sorry indeed to hear that Gissing [2] is unwell; and, as you seem to hint, somewhat gravely. Please express to him that it will give me very great pleasure to see him, and that if he only *will* let you convey him over I will surround him

[1] William James, his wife and his daughter Margaret were staying briefly with the novelist, before proceeding to Edinburgh where William delivered his first series of Gifford Lectures.

[2] On June 25 George Gissing wrote to his sister: "Wells and I went over to Rye and spent a night at Henry James's. He has a lovely old Georgian house, superbly furnished, looking over the shore to Winchelsea. Talked much of his acquaintance with Tourguenieff—interesting story."

with every solicitude in my power. But don't think of doing anything so arduous as to come for a couple of hours so dreadful a way. Come over in time for luncheon, of course, but stay and sleep—and do it *best*, on Tuesday or Wednesday—18th or 19th—of next week. I can put you both up for the night easily—and it's a far better business than the other system of—what shall I say?—all cry and no wool. Let us at least have as much wool as possible. I would propose tomorrow or Saturday were it not that 2 friends come down then till Monday. Do let me hear that this suits you and believe me yours always   HENRY JAMES

P.S. I wave my hands, mystically, over your roof-tree.

16

JAMES TO WELLS

Lamb House, Rye
June 20th 1901.

MY DEAR WELLS.

Will you very kindly attach to the enclosed Gissing's address and post it for me, receiving my thanks for the same? He has munificently sent me his beautiful book [1] and I desire to thank him, yet suppose him to be in the

[1] Probably *By the Ionian Sea*, a handsomely illustrated volume which Gissing had recently published.

act of quitting you. I had much pleasure and interest in your having brought him over—for highly sympathetic he seemed to me. But, by the same token, worn almost to the bone (of sadness.) Why *will* he do these things?

I hope peace and plenty hang over your house and settle in fact on your so frequently exposed head. I commend Mrs. Wells to your especial care (being particularly glad I kept you from her on Monday afternoon[)]; and am yours ever   HENRY JAMES

17

JAMES TO WELLS

Lamb House, Rye.
July 29: 1901

MY DEAR WELLS,

I am delighted with your news [1] (which I just return from a 10 days' absence to find;) and I much appreciate having it under your own hand and seal. I very heartily congratulate you, and I give Mrs. Wells the assurance of my abounding good wishes. I shower benedictions on the Boy, and wish I could wave a wand over his cradle, like a fairy in a pantomime. May all go well with you all, and better and better, precisely, *for* him. I much desire to look at him, and even—breathe it not to Mrs. Wells!—

[1] The birth of the Wells's first child, George Philip Wells.

to Hold him. I am really a great Babyholder—much better than penholder; as you see. I should like at any rate to feel of him. However, I must wait, for this, till there's more of him for the hand; though the quantity does already seem, by your account, most respectable.— Apropos of which does the quantity of poor Gissing continue to increase?[1] But you will—later on—tell me. I hope you have some better news of him. He rather haunts me. Yours always

HENRY JAMES

18

JAMES TO WELLS

Lamb House, Rye, Sussex.
January 20th, 1902.

MY DEAR WELLS,

Don't, I beseech you, measure the interest I've taken in your brilliant book (that is in the prior of the recent pair of them,) and don't measure any other decency or humanity of mine (in relation to anything that is yours,) by my late abominable and aggravated silence. You most handsomely sent me *Anticipations* when the volume appeared, and I was not able immediately to read it; I

---

[1] Wells tells in his *Experiment in Autobiography* how his wife, finding Gissing almost starved at the time of his visit to Spade House, had "set to work and fed him up—weighing him carefully at regular intervals—with the most marvellous results."

was bothered and preoccupied with many things, wished a free mind and an attuned ear for it, so let it wait till the right hour, knowing that neither you nor I would lose by the process. The right hour came, and I gave myself up—utterly, admirably up—to the charm; but the charm, on its side, left me so spent, as it were, with saturation, that I had scarce pulled myself round before the complications of Xmas set in, and the New Year's flood—in respect to correspondence—was upon me; which I've been till now buffeting and breasting. And then I was ashamed—and I'm ashamed still. That is the penalty of vice —one's shame disqualifies one for the company of virtue. Yet, all this latter time, I've taken the greatest pleasure in my still throbbing and responding sense of the book.

I found it then, I assure you, extraordinarily and unceasingly interesting. It's not that I haven't—hadn't— reserves and reactions, but that the great source of interest never failed: which great source was simply H. G. W. himself. You, really, come beautifully out of your adventure, come out of it immensely augmented and extended, like a belligerent who has annexed half-a-kingdom, with drums and trumpets and banners all sounding and flying. And this is because the thing, in our deadly day, is such a charming exhibition of complete freedom of mind. That's what I enjoyed in it— your intellectual disencumberedness; very interesting to behold as the direct fruit of training and observation. A gallant show altogether, and a gallant temper and a gallant tone. For the rest, you will be tired of hearing that, for vaticination, you, to excess, simplify. Besides, the phrophet (see how I recklessly spell him, to do him the greater honour!) *must*—I can't imagine a subtilizing prophet. At any rate I don't make you a reproach of simplifying, for if you hadn't I shouldn't have been able to understand you. But on the other hand I think your reader asks himself too much "Where is *life* in all this, life as I feel it and know it?" Subject of your speculations as it is, it is nevertheless too much left out. That comes partly from your fortunate youth—it's a more limited mystery for you than for the Methuselah who now addresses you. There's less of it with you to provide for, and it's less a perturber of your reckoning. There are for instance more kinds of people, I think, in the world— more irreducible kinds—than your categories meet. However, your categories do you, none the less, great honour, the greatest, worked out as they are; and I quite agree that, as before hinted, if one wants more life, there is Mr. Lewisham himself, of Spade House, exhaling it from every pore and in the centre of the picture. That is the great thing: he *makes*, Mr. Lewisham does, your heroic red-covered romance. It has to have a hero—and it has an irresistible one. Such is my criticism. I can't go further. I can't take you up in detail. I am under the charm. My world *is*, somehow, other; but I can't produce it. Besides, I don't want to. You can, and do, produce yours—so you've a right to talk. Finally, moreover, your book is full of truth and wit and sanity—that's where I mean you come out so well. I go to London next week for three months; but on my return, in May, I should like well to see you. What a season you must have had, with philosophy, poetry and the banker! I had a saddish letter from Gissing—but rumours of better things for him (I mean reviving powers,) have come to me, I don't quite know how, since. Conrad haunts Winchelsea, and Winchelsea (in discretion,) haunts Rye. So foot it up, and accept, at near one o'clock in the morning, the cordial good-night and general benediction of yours, my dear Wells, more than ever,

HENRY JAMES

19

JAMES TO WELLS

Lamb House, Rye.
Aug. 5th, 1902

MY DEAR WELLS.

I have found the Lady [1] extremely droll and curious, and all hung about with your characteristic wit, but I feel that (beyond thanking you with effusion for the handsome gift of her,) there is little I can say of her to you on these distant terms—in comparison with what I might say straight down your throat and holding you

---

[1] *The Sea Lady*, published at the end of July 1902.

meanwhile with mine eye. Therefore this closer relation cries aloud to be realised. It seems ages since we planned certain near meetings that have all too perversely never taken place. Let an early encounter wipe out the stain. *Do* let it, I very cordially urge you. Come over to luncheon some day, some early day, this month, and remain to dine and sleep. Dinner, the evening hour and sleep, are, to me, of the very essence of the propriety of the occasion. You will give me great pleasure by a liberal response. I greet your House, I bless your Babe, and last not least I send kindest regards to Mrs. Wells. Yours, cher grand confrère, always faithfully

HENRY JAMES

P.S. I should mention that the 12th and 13th are a little uncertain, and that a youth from an inebriate asylum at Battle comes to weep on my bosom one afternoon shortly subsequent. But I will square *him*. So you've only the 12th and 13th to leave out.

20

JAMES TO WELLS

Lamb House, Rye, Sussex.

Sept. 15, 1902

MY DEAR WELLS.

Forgive, please, my most accidental oblivions and delays and my present not less fortuitous brevity. A copy of my brother's book [1] leaves London for you to-morrow. I am delighted to be the means of your entering into possession of it. Yours always

HENRY JAMES.

P.S. Not the least dreadful of my oblivions has been to thank you for your princely present of your Lunar Series.[2] How can I sufficiently? I shall be doing it within a few days by fond and fascinated perusal. I write in a crisis of congestion.

H. J.

21

JAMES TO WELLS

Lamb House, Rye, Sussex
Sept. 20th, 1902.

MY DEAR WELLS.

It is all along of my execrable memory and the base futility thereof. And of *your* (I can't attempt, and LIVE, to let you wholly off,) too transcendant delicacy. If you had but returned, before you left, to the charming subject. But the solution is easy: it goes to you, with my fond blessing, this a.m. I trust it will reach you by tomorrow's post, as the book makes excellent Sunday

[1] Probably *The Varieties of Religious Experience*, William James's Gifford Lectures, which had just been published.

[2] *The First Men in the Moon*, published in November 1901.

reading.[1] And if, as I understand, you now have *two* of the other is it troubling you too odiously much to ask you to *return* me the second copy (I mean the one I caused to be addressed to you)? I am sure to have a lively need for it. All thanks in advance.

I am reading your Two Men [2] *à petites doses* as one sips (I suppose) old Tokay. Palpitations—painful—*versus* precipitation. But this catches the post. Yours always   HENRY JAMES

22

JAMES TO WELLS

Lamb House, Rye, Sussex.
September 23rd, 1902

MY DEAR WELLS,

All's well that ends well and everything is to hand. I thank you heartily for the same, and I have read the *Two Men*, dangling breathlessly at the tail of their tub while in the air and plying them with indiscreet questions while out of it. It is, the whole thing, stupenduous, but do you know what the main effect of it was on my cheeky consciousness? To make me sigh, on some such occasion,

[1] Probably a further allusion to William James's *The Varieties of Religious Experience.*

[2] Cavor and Bedford, the space travellers of *The First Men in The Moon.*

to *collaborate* with you, to intervene in the interest of—well, I scarce know what to call it: I must wait to find the right name when we meet. You can so easily avenge yourself by collaborating with *me*! Our mixture *would*, I think, be effective. I hope you are thinking of doing Mars—in some detail. Let me in *there*, at the right moment—or in other words at an early stage. I really shall, opportunity serving, venture to try to say two or three things to you about the Two Men—or rather not so much about them as about the cave of conceptions whence they issue. All I can say now however is that the volume *goes* like a bounding ball, that it is 12.30 a.m., and that I am goodnightfully yours,

HENRY JAMES.

23

JAMES TO WELLS

Lamb House, Rye, Sussex.

Oct. 7, 1902.

MY DEAR WELLS.

I feel that I should explain a little—even while I snatch at and tenderly nurture to a possible maturity any germ of interest and response in you. It is only that my sole and single way of perusing the fiction of Another is to *write it over*—even when most immortal—as I go. Write it over, I mean, *re*-compose it, in the light of my own high

F

sense of propriety and with immense refinements and em-
bellishments. I am so good in these cases as to accept the
subject *tel quel*—to take it over whole and make the best
of it. I took over so, for instance, in my locked breast,
the subject of Two Men etc. and the superstructure I
reared upon it had almost no resemblance to, or nothing
in common (*but* the subject!) with, yours. Unfortunately
yours had been made public first—which seemed hardly
fair. To obviate this injustice I think (and to secure an
ideal collaboration) I should be put in possession of your
work in its occult and pre-Pinkerite [1] state. Then I
should take it up and give it the benefit of my vision.
After which—as post-Pinkerite—it would have nothing
in common with the suggestive sheets received by me,
and yet we should have laboured in sweet unison. Think
of it well—sending me on, even, at your early convenience of "Shy and Shocked or the Burden of the Bash-
ful" [2]—or whatever you think of calling the so enticing
scheme you last hint at to me. Think of it, think of it;
and believe me your faithful finisher

HENRY JAMES

[1] James B. Pinker was one of Wells's, and James's literary agents.
[2] *Kipps*, on which Wells had been intermittently at work since
1899.

24

JAMES TO WELLS

Lamb House, Rye, Sussex.
November 15th, 1902.

MY DEAR WELLS,

It is too horribly long that I have neglected an interesting (for I can't say an interested) inquiry of yours—in your last note; and neglected precisely *because* the acknowledgment involved had to be an explanation. I have somehow, for the last month, not felt capable of explanations, it being my infirmity that when "finishing a book" (and that seems my chronic condition) my poor enfeebled cerebration becomes incapable of the least extra effort, however slight and simple. My correspondence then shrinks and shrinks—only the least explicit of my letters get themselves approximately written. And somehow it has seemed highly explicit to tell you that (in reply to your suggestive last) those wondrous and copious preliminary *statements*[1] (of my fictions that are to be,) don't really exist in any form in which they can be imparted. I think I know to whom you allude as having seen their semblance—and indeed their very substance; but in two exceptional (as it were) cases. In these cases

[1] James is here describing his dictated preliminary statements to his novels, two of which were preserved and posthumously published with the unfinished *The Sense of the Past* and *The Ivory Tower.*

what was seen was the statement drawn up on the basis
of the serialization of the work—drawn up in one case
with extreme detail and at extreme length (in 20,000
words!) [1] Pinker saw that: it referred to a long novel,
afterwards (this more than a year,) written and finished, but
not yet, to my great inconvenience, published; but it
went more than two years ago, to America, to the
Harpers, and there it remained and has probably been
destroyed. Were it here I would with pleasure transmit
it to you; for, though I say it who should not, it *was*, the
statement, full and vivid, I think, as a statement could be,
of a subject as worked out. Then CONRAD saw a shorter
one of the *Wings of the D[ove]*—also well enough in its
way, but only half as long and proportionately less
developed. *That* had been prepared so that the book
might be serialized in another American periodical, but
this wholly failed (what secrets and shames I reveal to
you!) and the thing (the book) was then written, the subject treated, on a more free and independent scale. But
that synopsis too has been destroyed; it was returned
from the U.S., but I had then no occasion to preserve it.
And evidently no fiction of mine can or *will* now be

---

[1] The 20,000-word statement was James's "Project of a Novel"
—his outline of *The Ambassadors* set down for Harper & Brothers.
Although the completed novel was sent to them in 1901 it was not
published until 1903 after serialisation in the *North American
Review*. In the interval James wrote and published *The Wings of
the Dove*. The full text of the outline for *The Ambassadors* was
published in *The Notebooks of Henry James* (ed. Matthiessen and
Murdock), 1947.

serialized; certainly I shall not again draw up detailed and explicit plans for unconvinced and ungracious editors; so that I fear I shall have nothing of that sort to show. A plan for *myself*, as copious and developed as possible, I always do draw up—that is the two documents I speak of were based upon, and extracted from, such a preliminary *private* outpouring. But this latter voluminous effusion is, ever, so extremely familiar, confidential and intimate—in the form of an interminable garrulous letter addressed to my own fond fancy—that, though I always, for easy reference, have it carefully typed, it isn't a thing I would willingly expose to any eye but my own. And even *then*, sometimes, I shrink! So there it is. I am greatly touched by your respectful curiosity, but I haven't, you see, anything coherent to produce. Let me promise however that if I ever do, within any calculable time, address a manifesto to the dim editorial mind, you shall certainly have the benefit of a copy. Candour compels me to add that that consummation has now become unlikely. It is too wantonly expensive a treat to them. In the first place they will none of me, and in the second the relief, and greater intellectual dignity, so to speak, of working on one's own scale, one's own line of continuity and in one's own absolutely independent *tone*, is too precious to me to be again forfeited. Pardon my too many words. I only add that I hope the domestic heaven bends blue above you. Yours, my dear Wells, always,

HENRY JAMES

25

JAMES TO WELLS

Lamb House, Rye, Sussex.

November 18th, 1902

MY DEAR WELLS.

Very good your idea that J. B. P[inker] [1] may be able to recover the precious draft from the Harpers. My fatalistic mind hadn't even entertained the possibility. But I will see him about it—I go to London on Thursday for 4 or 5 days (but to be spent mostly indeed in the country,) and if the thing has not long since been incinerated you shall still be placed in (possibly rather bored) relation with it. But I fear for its mere existence.

Oh, I too have corresponded with Ouida [2] (though only on the relations of the sexes,) and it has "ended badly"—as badly as one of my novels. Ouida—most Fatuous of Females—*does* end badly, as a correspondent. Ouida *will* end badly, as a Female. The rumour is (the belief,) that she surrenders herself periodically, poor lady, to—vivisection. But enough. (Destroy this, please!)—

[1] Pinker did not recover the scenario or statement for *The Ambassadors*; the manuscript remained in America and passed into the hands of a private collector.

[2] This is apparently an ironic reference to the anti-vivisection activities of Louise Ramé (Ouida), the novelist, with whom James had a slight acquaintance. Ouida was writing to Wells about *Mankind in the Making*, which had just begun its serial appearance in the *Fortnightly Review*.

I congratulate you heartily on your Town House (I feel so greatly the benefit myself of a microscopic pied-à-terre in London.) I go up early in January for four months, and you must make me (respectfully) free of it. Clement's Inn, even that *was*, sounds thrilling, at least that *was*. I don't see the *Fortnightly*, or go to the Cobden Club; but I live for your agglomerated lucubrations. Continue then to agglomerate. Yours always

HENRY JAMES

26

JAMES TO WELLS

Lamb House, Rye, Sussex
October 14th, 1903.

MY DEAR WELLS,

Your generous and beautiful letter is not, I feel, a thing I can "thank" you for—that form is associated with much meaner occasions and much slighter services. And I can scarce send you back, adequately, the reflection of the glow you have produced in a bosom in which, mostly, any such fire languishes for lack of fuel. Therefore what *can* I do? Well, I can give you my word for the pleasure it was to hear from you so handsomely—to hear from you, above all, that, digger and explorer of so-much deeper and duskier mines, you still get something *out* of my comparatively shallow pit. It's a luxury to be read

with a certain intelligence—and the quality must make
up for the quantity. My book [1] has been out upwards of
a month and, not emulating your 4,000, has sold, I believe,
to the extent of 4 copies. In America it is doing better—
promises to reach 400. But I count your letter as, for a
result, at least a thousand. It makes me want to see you
again—soon—though I always want to do that; and
some time during the autumn this must be managed.
Only give me time and I will come over and spend three
days at the Folkestone hostelry and interview you constantly. I speak of the F.H. because I am so inapt as a
non-"paying" guest. I always insist on paying, and you
wouldn't let me do that. At present I am beset, here, as I
have been all summer, with guests who stay, but don't
pay, and who keep me from writing a long article that I
have promised to a heavy periodical,[2] and from reading
over the books, even, necessary to the production of the
same; also from finishing a novel [3] the delivery of which
is contracted for by Nov. 30th; all of which represents a
complication of anxieties that has had for effect to make
me go on *keeping* your great little volume [4] for some day
of sweet, free religious attention that, on its side, goes on
postponing itself. But it will come as soon as my article

[1] *The Ambassadors*.

[2] Probably his article on d'Annunzio published in the *Quarterly
Review*, April 1904.

[3] *The Golden Bowl*.

[4] Presumably *Mankind in the Making*, published in September
1903.

is written and the victims of my hospitality are also in some way finished. I hold you meantime in grateful affection, and, with renewed blessings on your house and its " main factors," am yours, my dear Wells, always

HENRY JAMES

27

JAMES TO WELLS

Lamb House, Rye, Sussex.

Nov. 24. 1903.

MY DEAR WELLS.

Very gratifying to me your letter, and in nothing more than by its rosy light projected on your second-born.[1] The light is cast back from that pink identity, very handsomely and enviably, on you and Mrs. Wells and on your whole clustered existence; and you all "compose" together as happily as could be desired. But I wish indeed I could just now see my way to feeling myself, more completely, "in the picture" with you. It's sad to say, but I fear I can't leave home this coming month—I shall have to wait for my pilgrimage, till the complication of Xmas is over. I have in prospect a very time-devouring liability for that equivocal anniversary—which I always seem condemned, here, to spend at home—at the receipt of the genial domestic vampire, and which creates a desert of

[1] Frank Richard Wells.

apprehension, preparation and prostration before it and behind. Have a little further patience with me, all the same, for I renew my vow to you that the Pavilion at Folkestone shall know me, and Spade House concomitantly, on the very earliest manageable date. I am trying and above all tried—but I am not false—least of all as yours, your wife's and your sons' very constantly

HENRY JAMES

28

JAMES TO WELLS

Lamb House, Rye, Sussex.
Nov. 27th, 1903.

[*Dictated.*]

MY DEAR WELLS.

Forgive my addressing you with this fierce legibility— the only course open to me for ideal promptitude. I go up to town in an hour or two for three or four days, and am liable to be plunged there into complications that will have my correspondence much at their mercy. Also I am almost indecently eager to converse with you, however briefly and barely for the present, on the interesting theme you broach. Yet my eagerness, alas, doesn't proceed from my being able to flood the subject for you with any rosy light—or indeed with any "light" whatever worthy of the name. You touch on a matter as to which

I have been myself long helplessly at sea, as to which I still sit in darkness and almost in despair. My little affairs *are* little affairs, and thereby different from yours, who have big interests and big possibilities at stake; so I have gone on feebly and vaguely, seeking no aid even while feeling that my case *can* be, in some degree or other, bettered. J. B. P[inker] has done for me, the last five or six years, whatever has been done in America, and, strange as it may appear to you, I have (with my immemorial absence, detachment, and practical idiocy,) no attachments there save through him. Yet I have all the while felt him but little "in it", in that multitudinous field, compared with someone or other who should be on the spot; and this is so true that I am planning (though still with characteristic debility and imbecility) to visit the scene itself some time next year, largely in order to see if I may not somehow mend my meagre market. I have had relations, all my days, with but three American houses: Houghton, Mifflin and Co. in Boston; Ch[arles] Scribner's Sons and the Harpers in New York. I have been too long away, and am too incredibly little informed, to know if there be any younger and better blood about the place than I so refer to; but I take these people for the most traditionally-respectable, most consecrated by time and whatever other mystic graces. There are also of course the Appletons, whom you know, and who are a "big" house, but with whom I have never had anything to do; and there are the murderous Macmillans, in the person of G. P.

Brett, their American manager, with whom I have had as little as possible. Such is my homely, humble tale. The "literary agent" does, I believe, exist there, and it is precisely to discover him that I myself desire. He has, I blush to confess, never approached me of his own free motion. Save by some vague, long-ago, forgotten circular or two. My old friend W[illiam] D[ean] H[owells] is, and has been for long years, the personal (literary) property of the Harpers, who appear to have found, always, more or less largely, their account in him, as he has found his in *them*. He has been kind to me about one or two matters with the said H's, but though I have given him a little the opportunity to name to me somebody, in his purview, who could "act" for me, it has not appeared to strike him that there was anyone worth his naming. My impression is that he is able to "act", consummately, for himself, and that such fifth wheels to his coach are not very present to him. With which rather too many words I fear I assist you but little. My sense of the matter for you, to be frank, is that you would do by no means amiss to visit the complicated scene yourself and bring your own masterly intelligence directly to bear. You will find this illuminating, I am sure, in all sorts of ways; and it strikes me in general that a man, over here, who has, as you have, a public over there endowed with large possibilities of extension, ought, both in his interest and theirs, to look at them more nearly face to face and get in a manner to know them. If I wind *myself* up to the miracle of going, however, it will not be for a good many months to come—toward the end of next year if at all. I have been rather hoping that J.B.P. knew and felt the limitations of his American range; but if he is *without* the consciousness of sin he is not, I fear, likely to regenerate in the fashion I have also, with limp optimism, been praying for. In a word, go yourself! Which you will say, is "cool" of me while I crouch here! So I won't pretend to conceal from you that I do just, cynically, desire and invoke your braver example! See what you have brought on yourself. And believe me yours ever

HENRY JAMES

29

JAMES TO WELLS

Lamb House, Rye, Sussex.
January 24th, 1904.

MY DEAR WELLS.

You have done me the honour more than once to compliment me very handsomely on my faculty, such as it is, of Expression, but I think I must have won from you by this time at least an equal tribute to my power of silence. I won't pretend to enumerate the attenuating circumstances that cluster round my fault—I find it a simpler course to admit frankly that I have been graceless and abominable. The absurd part of the matter is, too, that I've *wanted*, day after day, to write—wanted to quite intensely from the day I read your two so munificently-conferred books. The more distinctively prophetic of the two has been the same "intellectual treat" to me as its predecessors; I mean that it has affected me, in the same way, as a record of romantic adventure of which You are the Hero. As such M[*ankind*] *in the* M[*aking*] thrills and transports me—so little does the interest ever flag that hangs about your brilliant gallantry in the sorest stress— about your dire exposure, your miraculous resource and your final hairbreadth escape. For you do escape, thank heaven, for other palpitations to come—the sense of which is one of the consolations of my life. Seriously, I found myself singularly subjugated by your volume and in abject agreement with its main thesis—which nothing, it seems to me, can stand up against. And the humanity and lucidity and ingenuity, the pluck and perception and patience and humour of the whole thing place you before me as, simply, one of the benefactors of our race. But my sense, too, is really all summed up in my vision, as I say, of the essential gallantry of your mind. It becomes, as one reads, inordinately objective, heroic, sympathetic, D'Artagnanesque.

Of the little Tales in t'other book [1] I read one every night regularly, after going to bed—they had only the defect of hurrying me prematurely to my couch. They were each to me as a substantial coloured sweet or bonbon

[1] *Twelve Stories and a Dream* (1903).

—one pink, the other crimson, the other a golden amber or a tender green, which I just allowed to *melt* lollipop-wise, upon my imaginative tongue. Some of the colours seemed to me perhaps prettier than the others, as some oranges are the larger and some the smaller, in any dozen. But I (excuse me!) sucked *all* the oranges.

And with all this experience of you I had, in its season, that of knowing, in an imperfect roundabout way, that you made that admirable effort for poor Gissing *in extremis* [1]—my failure to thank you for which at the time must have affected you as an ugly note. When I say to "thank" you I mean—well, I mean *just* that, after all—though you may very well not have noticed whether I was audible or not. I was in truth, at the time you must have returned, audible only as a groaner and even curser under the discipline of the gout-fiend—having had, shortly after the New Year, to tumble into bed with a violent attack, and then to spend tiresome days in my chair, which I have only lately quitted. These conditions made writing, for a long spell, a highly avoidable effort. And *now* I can't write of Gissing with any pertinence, for I am concerned only with the prospect, some day not too long hence, of asking you, face to face, for the story of your surely most dismal, as it was a most generous, pilgrimage. I wish I could name the day for this by telling

---

[1] Wells had gone to Gissing in St. Jean-de-Luz, when word reached him that his friend was dying, and remained with him during his last illness. See *Experiment in Autobiography*, VIII, 3.

you that I am myself ready (under a luckily brighter star,) to peregrinate to Folkstone—but I should have to strain the point of veracity to do so. My damnable gout attack has knocked my time into Smithereens; I am obliged to go to London next week, for some stay, and I fear that this is the only winter journey that, in my actual conditions, I can aspire to. What has become meanwhile of your own London pied-à-terre—and is there no chance of my seeing you *there*? I shall really be in town (105 Pall Mall, S.W.) till Easter—whereby can't you cultivate some simultaneity? I go to America to "look after my interests" on Aug. 24th, and from Easter till then shall not budge (further than Folkestone,) I devoutly hope, from *this* spot. All of which means that I should like immensely, and much rather sooner than later, to see you. I send meanwhile more and more comprehensive salutations to your house and am yours, my dear Wells, very cordially and constantly   HENRY JAMES

30

JAMES TO WELLS

105 *Pall Mall, S.W.*

14.2.04.

MY DEAR WELLS.

I am horribly haunted by the sense that I failed somehow, at the time, to answer your last genial note. I fully and intensely meant to—but I have an uncanny absence of recollection of the act itself, and, if so—I mean if no response did break my raw silence—I grovel before you most apologetically. You kindly asked me to join you at some club banquet—and then you wrote me another fact about it; and the more I brood on the matter the more convinced I am that the responsive pen must, by some combination of interruptions now irrecoverable, have been dashed from my hand. But, with all kindest thanks, I can't go, *couldn't* have gone. I never go to banquets where there are speeches, however informal—it's a dreary little "rule" I had long [ago] to make. I hope with all my heart that my silence hasn't incommoded you. I stay here till about April 5th: over Easter. I'm very sorry you have ceased to flirt with the metropolis. She is not an honest woman; but a discreet measure of her intercourse is enjoyable; at least by yours ever

HENRY JAMES

3 1

JAMES TO WELLS

Reform Club, Pall Mall, S.W.
Feb. 17th, 1904.

MY DEAR WELLS.

No—the mystic empty envelope *didn't* proceed—for a wonder!—from that seat of every inadvertance known to

G

myself as my precarious consciousness; and responsible as I feel in a general way for Rye, its postmark, and its products, I confess myself unimaginatively powerless before the mystery. It's a case rather for Conan Doyle. But I *did* send you some 3 or 4 days ago (from here) if not a full envelope at least a partially fed one. Yours ever

HENRY JAMES

32

JAMES TO WELLS

Lamb House, Rye, Sussex.

May 8th, 1904.

MY DEAR WELLS.

My old friend W. D. Howells,[1] the American novelist, is staying with his daughter, at Folkestone, and I said to him a day or two ago (on his passing a couple of nights here,) that you and Mrs. Wells were the principal attraction of that neighbourhood and that I felt it a great pity they shouldn't know you. He said they should be delighted to, in fact particularly desired it—and I said I would write and ask you if you wouldn't perhaps go and

[1] Wells entertained Howells at Sandgate on this occasion, and later, during a trip to the United States, was asked by him to a luncheon, to which Mark Twain was also invited. Howells described Wells as "a cockney of a brave spirit, who is socialistic in his expectations of the future and boldly owns to having been a dry goods clerk in his own past."

see them. He is the dearest and most genial of men, and his daughter is altogether charming. They are at Devonshire House, 2 Clifton Road, and I should be delighted if you could pay them this amiable attention. If you and Mrs. Wells *do* call and ask them to tea I shall moreover have the luxury of hearing from them about you, and your latest news will be much of a pleasure to yours and your wife's always

HENRY JAMES

33

JAMES TO WELLS

Lamb House, Rye, Sussex.
May 10th, 1904.

MY DEAR WELLS.

Very beautiful to me, in its so generous appreciation, your little word about my "critical effort" in the last "Quarterly" [1]—and I thank you for it as with tears in my eyes.

I wrote you on Saturday last asking you to very kindly go and see my old friend W. D. Howells (the American novelist) who is at Folkestone (2 Clifton Road)—only over next Sunday, I think; but I fear my letter will have found you in London, and if you are remaining there any

---

[1] The article on d'Annunzio, reprinted in *Notes on Novelists*, to which James had alluded in an earlier letter (see p. 88).

time the possibility in question will have dropped by
your absence—which I shall quite understand without
explanations. But you would have liked—or perhaps still
will—dear old Howells—and possibly Mrs. Wells would
have been able to see his daughter, who is also a dear. But
the spiced cup of London is doubtless still at your lips!

Yours, my dear Wells, always and ever

HENRY JAMES

34

JAMES TO WELLS

Lamb House, Rye, Sussex.

Saturday [*June*, 1904]

The young lady, my dear Wells, is *Mildred* Howells—
and it [is] as such that I would inscribe any offering made
her—I do so hate our twopenny Anglosaxon "Miss."
Though of course, as she has no sister, you may perfectly
address anything to her Miss H. She is a charming flower
of "Puritanism"—very intelligent and subtle; though,
alas, apparently destitute, almost, of physical substance:
which is an indispensable basis for complete charm.
Howells himself is indeed a man of gold—for the milk
of human kindness, humour, modesty and other things
besides. We will talk of them later!

Yours ever

HENRY JAMES

35

JAMES TO WELLS

Lamb House, Rye, Sussex.
June 10th, 1904.

MY DEAR WELLS.

This [is] an awful revelation of inadvertance and frivolity.

Miss Howells, 1 *Clarges St. W.*

will reach her till the 15th a.m. But c/o Harper and Bros. will always reach them—H. and Bros. I mean, 45 Albemarle St. W. Everything is quickly forwarded from there as they move about, and I am yours utterly abashed and discredited

HENRY JAMES

P.S. Oh, the Brienz of June, the high Alpine meadows and the heartbreaking memories of my lost youth. Happy adolescents you twain!

36

JAMES TO WELLS

Lamb House, Rye, Sussex.
November 19th, 1905.

MY DEAR WELLS

If I take up time and space with telling you why I have not *sooner* written to thank you for your magnificent bounty, I shall have, properly, to steal it from my letter, my letter itself; a much more important matter. And yet I *must* say, in three words, that my course has been inevitable and natural. I found your first munificence here on returning from upwards of 11 months in America, toward the end of July—returning to the mountain of Arrears produced by almost a year's absence and (superficially, thereby,) a year's idleness. I recognized, even from afar (I had already done so) that the Utopia [1] was a book I should desire to read only in the right conditions of *coming* to it, coming with luxurious freedom of mind, rapt surrender of attention, adequate honours, for it of every sort. So, not bolting it like the morning paper and sundry, many, other vulgarly importunate things, and knowing, moreover, I had already shown you that though I was slow I was safe, and even certain, I "came to it" only a short time since, and surrendered my-

[1] Wells's *A Modern Utopia*, published, like *Kipps*, in 1905.

self to it absolutely. And it was while I was at the bottom
of the crystal well that Kipps suddenly appeared, thrust-
ing his honest and inimitable head over the edge and
calling down to me, with his note of wondrous truth, that
he had business with me above. I took my time, however,
there below (though "below" be a most improper figure
for your sublime and vertiginous heights,) and achieved
a complete saturation; after which, reascending and making out things again, little by little, in the dingy air of the
actual, I found Kipps, in his place, awaiting me—and
from his so different but still so utterly coercive embrace I
have just emerged. It was really very well he was there,
for I found (and it's even a little strange,) that I could
read *you* only—AFTER YOU—and don't at all see whom
else I could have read. But now that this is so I don't see
either, my dear Wells, how I can "write" you about these
things—they make me want so infernally to talk with
you, to see you at length. Let me tell you, however,
simply, that they have left me prostrate with admiration,
and that you are, for me, more than ever, the most
interesting "literary man" of your generation—in fact,
the only interesting one. These things do you, to my
sense, the highest honour, and I am lost in amazement at
the diversity of your genius. As in everything you do
(and especially in these three last Social Imaginations) [1]
it is the quality of your intellect that primarily (in the
Utopia) obsesses me and reduces me—to that degree that

[1] *Anticipations, Mankind in the Making*, and *A Modern Utopia*.

even the colossal dimensions of your Cheek (pardon the
term that I don't in the least invidiously apply,) fails to
break the spell. Indeed your Cheek is positively the very
sign and stamp of your genius, valuable to-day, as you
possess it, beyond any other instrument or vehicle, so
that when I say it doesn't break the charm, I probably
mean that it largely constitutes it, or constitutes the force:
which is the force of an irony that no one else among us
begins to have—so that we are starving, in our enormities
and fatuities, for a sacred satirist (the satirist *with* irony—
as poor dear old Thackeray was the satirist without it,)
and you come, admirably, to save us. There are too many
things to say—which is so exactly why I can't write.
Cheeky, cheeky, cheeky is *any* young man at Sandgate's
offered Plan for the life of Man—but so far from thinking
that a disqualification of your book, I think it is positively
what makes the performance heroic. I hold, with you,
that it is only by our each contributing Utopias (the
cheekier the better,) that anything will come, and I think
there is nothing in the book truer and happier than your
speaking of this struggle of the rare yearning individual
toward that suggestion as one of the certain assistances of
the future. Meantime you set a magnificent example—
of *caring*, of feeling, of seeing, above all, and of suffering
from, and with, the shockingly sick actuality of things.
Your epilogue tag in italics, strikes me as of the highest,
of an irresistible and touching beauty. Bravo, bravo, my
dear Wells!

And now, coming to Kipps, what am I to say about Kipps but that I am ready, that I am compelled, utterly to *drivel* about him? He is not so much a masterpiece as a mere born gem—you having, I know not how, taken a header straight down into mysterious depths of observation and knowledge, I know not which and where, and come up again with this rounded pearl of the diver. But of course you know yourself how immitigably the thing is done—it is of such a brilliancy of *true* truth. I really think that you have done, at this time of day, two particular things for the first time of their doing among us. (1) You have written the first closely and intimately, the first intelligently and consistently ironic or satiric novel. In everything else there has always been the sentimental or conventional interference, the interference of which Thackeray is full. (2) You have for the very first time treated the English "lower middle" class, etc., without the picturesque, the grotesque, the fantastic and romantic interference, of which Dickens, e.g., is so misleadingly, of which even George Eliot is so deviatingly, full. You have handled its vulgarity in so scientific and historic a spirit, and seen the whole thing all in its *own* strong light. And then the book has, throughout, such extraordinary life; everyone in it, without exception, and every piece and part of it, is so vivid and sharp and *raw*. Kipps himself is a diamond of the first water, from start to finish, exquisite and radiant; Coote is consummate, Chitterlow magnificent (the whole first evening with Chitterlow

perhaps the most brilliant thing in the book—unless that
glory be reserved for the way the entire matter of the
shop is done, including the admirable image of the boss.)
It all in fine, from cover to cover, does you the greatest
honour, and if we had any other than skin-deep criticism
(very stupid, too, at [th]at,) it would have immense
recognition. I repeat that these things have made me
want greatly to see you. Is it thinkable to you that you
might come over at this ungenial season, for a night,—
some time before Xmas? Could you, would you? I
should immensely rejoice in it. I am here till Jan. 31st—
when I go up to London for three months. I go away,
probably, for four or five days at Xmas—and I go away
for next Saturday–Tuesday. But apart from those dates I
would await you with rapture.

And let me say just one word of attenuation of my
(only apparent) meanness over the *Golden Bowl*.[1] I was
in America when that work appeared, and it was published there in 2 vols, and in very charming and readable
form, each vol. but moderately thick and with a legible,
handsome, large-typed page. But there came over to me
a copy of the London issue, fat, vile, small-typed, horrific,
prohibitive, that so broke my heart that I vowed I
wouldn't, for very shame, disseminate it, and I haven't,
with that feeling, had a copy in the house or sent one to a
single friend. I wish I had an American one at your dis-

[1] *The Golden Bowl* was published in the United States in 1904,
in England in 1905.

position—but I have been again and again depleted of all ownership in respect to it. You are very welcome to the British brick if you, at this late day, will have it. I greet Mrs. Wells and the Third Party very cordially and am yours, my dear Wells, more than ever,

HENRY JAMES

37

WELLS TO JAMES

Spade House, Sandgate.

Jan. 25. 06.

MY DEAR JAMES.

I have booked a cabin on the *Carmania* for March 27th. Heaven knows when I shall return, and I am going to write loose large articles mingled with impressions of *The Future in America* (no less). I shall be very grateful if you can give me letters to any typical people. I suppose you know no one in Salt Lake City? If I could get any insight into the social life of that place I would brave that long extra journey from Chicago very willingly. I want to see something of the social effects of the varying divorce laws and there perhaps Miss Edith Wharton [1] will talk to me—you promised me her. I shall stay some days in *New York* coming and going, I shall make a desperate

[1] Mrs Wharton was to describe Wells in her reminiscences as the "most stirring and responsive of talkers."

attempt on your brother, spend a day or so in Boston and I'm resolved in Chicago and Washington. The rest is as God wills. I shall be very glad if I could be put up as a temporary member in any New York Club in which there are literary people to be met and perhaps you could think of a sponsor for me.

Forgive these large demands. I'm too greedy to see and hear to be modest.

Yours ever

H. G. WELLS

A letter on the *Golden Bowl* impends. These gross demands in the meanwhile.

38

JAMES TO WELLS

Lamb House, Rye, Sussex.

Aug. 9th, 1906.

MY DEAR WELLS.

I shall be very frantically brief in thanking you for your genial letter.

I go on Saturday next to Folkestone—to spend Sunday with a pair of American cousins who are perching at the Lear Hotel. *But* I foresee that I should (*shall*) be able to take out, with ease or comfort, during that time, no sufficient piece to foregather (with any fulness of felicity) with *you*. Howsomever, I should be able to come on Saturday week—the 18th—if that is convenient to you; this will I do with pleasure and spend the Sunday, if I hear from you affirmatively. Then we shall have time to ourselves, and I yearn to converse with you. Kindly say to Mrs. Wells, with my best remembrance, that my dietary is the *easiest* mere tissue of feeble negatives. I eat but little here below, but I eat that little long [1]—and it's a little of the absolute obvious. Yours and hers, my dear Wells, most truly

HENRY JAMES

P.S. I should reach you toward 5.30.

39

JAMES TO MRS. WELLS

Lamb House, Rye, Sussex.
Aug. 15th, 1906.

DEAR MRS. WELLS.

Your kind note gives me great pleasure and adds to my impatience for next Saturday, when I shall rejoicingly

---

[1] A variation on Goldsmith's lines in "Edwin and Angelina":
> Man wants but little here below,
> Nor wants that little long.

James is alluding to his habit of "Fletcherizing"—his adoption of a fad of that period introduced by Horace Fletcher, which called for prolonged and leisurely chewing of food.

present myself by a certain 4.6 from here, which is the train reaching Folkestone Central at 5.25. Delightful to me is the sense of the end of my grotesque Years of Delay to tread your charming halls. I found it delightful even to look down on them last Sunday—that is on the fore-shortened crown of them—from beside the little Funicular station. I adored your Location, as they say in the U.S. (and as Wells of course now says,) on the spot. I don't *arrive*, however, I take it, by Funicular, and my train gets to Sandgate via Sandling Junction at 5.24. I am a little vague as to the Shorncliffe alternative, but shall assume Sandling if I hear nothing from you otherwise, and am, with all greetings to H.G., yours and his most truly

HENRY JAMES

40

JAMES TO WELLS

Lamb House, Rye, Sussex.

10.11.06

MY DEAR WELLS.

I think I have already brought it home to you that I am eternally backward and belated and inapt to write, as in the newspapers, "Out to Day," at the head of my "literary opinions." Reading a book of yours is a great circumstance and solemnity—a great experience—to me

and surrounded with grave forms and rites of which my
delayed resort to consequent speech is an essential part.
I *taste* you immensely as I take you in—that is I go on
tasting and tasting, and it is as if, while this lasts, I had
my mouth very full. So I have been tasting your Comet-
ary Tale [1]—every inch and ounce of it: a very curious
business. You *interest* me intensely and that work has
done so on every page, having, as it seems to me, extraordinary force and sincerity. You have *force* as really
no one has it, and in the fashion of some irresistible
chemical dissolvent, so that reading you is really being
"acted upon" in a manner that is akin to conscience and
anguish. I don't find your work—or at least this one—
as projected an artistic fact, quite, as it is my habit to
yearn to find suchlike—one doesn't, in it, take refuge,
(one *can't*,) in the waiting-room of The Crematorium,
with a saddened sense of the dread Process going on
adjacently—one is in presence of the heated oven and one
hears and feels the roar and the scorch of the flames.
That is your Book—magnificently crematory, in other
words magnificently direct and real (though perhaps with
too little of the waiting room.) However, it isn't of any
" too little " I am moved to speak to you, but of the immense value I find in your power and truth and sincerity
(this last of the highest order:) it is all of huge positive
worth, a golden vessel which you flourish about with a
hand of inimitable freedom. The interesting thing in the

[1] *In the Days of the Comet*, published in September 1906.

painter of life, or storyteller, as they say, is his *kind of consciousness* and I revel in yours (which is of the rarest,) *all* the while; and in your expression of it *most* of the same. You have expressed that of your pre-cometary world (a splendid statement in its way I really think) better, to my sense—and inevitably—than that of the sequel to the Cataclysm; but I have surrendered to the whole, ever so gratefully, and the gallantry of your post-cataclysmal view has in fact its own wild charm. You have made me want much to see you again, and we must pull this off. The 2 or 3 "reviews" I've seen of you have been ignobly stupid—but I would have stayed your hand from taking up the one in the *Times*—though you did so with an excellent manner.[1] The thing was too utterly on the *basis* of stupidity and puerility. I greet Mrs. Wells and dream of Spade House on such a day as this—as these—have been. Always yours

HENRY JAMES

[1] *The Times Literary Supplement* reviewed *In the Days of the Comet* on 17 September 1906. Wells commented on this review in a letter printed in that journal on 28 September.

41

JAMES TO WELLS

Lamb House, Rye, Sussex.

Nov. 8, 1906

MY DEAR WELLS.

I came back last night from five days in London to find your so generously-given "America," [1] and I have done nothing today but thrill and squirm with it and vibrate to it almost feverishly and weep over it almost profusely (this last, I mean, for intensity of mere emotion and interest.) But the difficulty is that I am too dazzled by your extraordinary, your (to me) fascinating, intellectual energy for all the *judgment* of you that I should like to be able to command. The mere sight and sense and sound of your prodigious *reactions* before the spectacle of all actualities, combined with your power of making all those actualities—by a turn of the hand—consist of amazing, fermenting, immeasurable passionate "questions" and social issues, comes near affecting me as the performance of a "strong man" or a conjurer, (juggler;) seems to show you playing with your subject and its parts as with the articles those *virtuosi* cause to rebound and fly about. This amounts to saying that what primarily flies in my face in *these* things of yours is *you* and your so amazingly

[1] *The Future in America*, published by Chapman and Hall in 1906.

H

active and agile intellectual personality—I may even say
your sublime and heroic cheek—which I can't resist for
the time, can't *sufficiently* resist, to allow me to feel (as
much as I want to,) that you tend always to simplify
overmuch (that is as to large *particulars*—though in
effect I don't think you do here as to the whole.) But
what am I talking about, when just this ability and impulse to simplify—so vividly—is just what I all yearn-
ingly envy you?—I who was accursedly born to touch
nothing save to complicate it. Take these fevered lines
tonight then simply for a sign of my admiring, panting,
more or less gasping impression and absorption of your
book. When I think of the brevity of the process, of the
direct and immediate experience, from which it springs,
the intensity and superiority of the projection of the
realization, leave me, I confess, quite wonderstricken, and
I ask myself if such a quantity of *important* observation—
so *many* of such—have ever before sprung into life under
so concentrated a squeeze. I think not, and your vividness
and your force and your truth, and your caught and
seized images, aspects, characteristics and conditions are
infinitely remarkable, for all your precipitation. I
seemed to see, for myself, while I was there, absolutely
no profit in scanning or attempting to sound the future—
the present being so hugely fluid and the direction (beyond mere space and quantity and motion so incalculable
—as to the *whole*;) and yet here you come and throw
yourself *all* on the future, and leave out almost alto-

gether the America of my old knowledge; leave out all
sorts of things, and I am gripped and captured and over-
whelmingly beguiled. It comes of your admirable communicative passion for the idea, and from your wealth of
ideas, and from your way of making intensely interesting
each one that you touch. I think you, frankly,—or think
the whole thing—too *loud*, as if the country shouted at
you, hurrying past, every hint it had to give and you
yelled back your comment on it; but also, frankly, I think
the right and the only way to utter many of the things
you are delivered of *is* to yell them—it's a yelling country,
and the voice must pierce or dominate; and *my* semitones,
in your splendid clashing of the cymbals (and *theirs*,) will
never be heard.[1] But there are still more things to say
than I can so much as glance at, and I've only wanted to
put to you, before I go to bed, that your book is, to my
vision, extraordinarily full and rich and powerful and
worthy, for all its fine fury of procedure—or perhaps
just by reason of the same—of the vast uncomfortable
subject. How glad you must be to have cast it from you!
I don't know where this will find you—amid what
blooming of citrons—but may it find you safely and
assure you both that I am, as by communication, breathlessly yours

HENRY JAMES

[1] James's book of American impressions, *The American Scene*,
was offered to English readers by the same publisher in 1907.

42

WELLS TO JAMES

20. iii. 07

MY DEAR JAMES.

I've read the *American Scene* and again I've read *in* the *American Scene* and I've reread Richmond (which is one of the most wonderful things you have done) and Baltimore several times and I found very little to say to you except something in the way of a more respectful salutation than even I've made before on these occasions.

The things are so completely done, the atmospheres return, elucidated; once again I have visited Washington and the White House. You take the thing (as you said) at the opposite pole to my attack, you make it a criticism of life and manners—things I have had only incidental dealings with—you take the whole thing as an ineffectual civilisation and judge it with so temperate and informed a decisiveness. But I wish there was a Public worthy of you—and me. After the book is closed and I have gloated again in the still almost incredible marvel of a cover "uniform" with mine, I do get this gleam of discontent. How much will they get out of what you have got in?

Xaver

Yours ever,

H. G. WELLS

43

JAMES TO MRS. WELLS

Lamb House, Rye, Sussex.

July 28th, 1908

DEAR MRS. WELLS,

Your note is so kind that I really require courage to say in return that I fear it won't do for me to leave home just now. I am the centre of a wide and *general* assault of relations—relays of cousins pour down from London (in addition to nearer elements of consanguinity) these weeks being the thick of the American season and my poor house, apparently, the most frequent European objective. Add to it that I am frantically occupied on lines independent of this, and that having people constantly with me causes such a sacrifice of time that when I put in delightful days abroad as well the carnival seems fatally complete and sacred pledges go under. This, dear Mrs. Wells, is my woeful truthful tale—it's really of a desperate difficulty to me to abandon my post during these midsummer weeks. This is almost each year the case—and just now I find it particularly unadvisable to go forth while my brother is with me.[1] His wife and Peggy depart

[1] William James had early discerned a fellow-pragmatist in Wells, and in 1905 his enthusiasm for *A Modern Utopia* had led him to write a letter to Wells about his "unparallelled and transcendant virtues." When William visited Lamb House in 1908, he and Wells became firm friends, who found each other's temperament

(for two or three weeks, or more) on Friday, but he stays
on longer—and we meet the rest of the fray together.

---

and outlook immensely congenial. William particularly enjoyed a reference to Chesterton in Wells's letter of welcome.
Aware of his admiration for this celebrity, who was James's next-
door neighbour, Wells noted that as he looked across the marsh,
it appeared to him that the outline of Rye was altered "by a remarkable bulge . . . in its contour," which "seems to distend post-
prandially." In his *Experiment in Autobiography* (p. 538) Wells
tells how it finally fell to him to make William and Chesterton
acquainted. "I once saw Henry James quarrelling with his brother,"
Wells relates. "He had lost his calm; he was terribly unnerved.
He appealed to me, to me of all people, to adjudicate on what was
and what was not permissible behaviour in England. William was
arguing about it in an indisputably American accent, with an indecently naked reasonableness. I had come to Rye with a car to
fetch William James and his daughter to my home at Sandgate.
William had none of Henry's passionate regard for the polish upon
the surfaces of life and he was immensely excited by the fact that
in the little Rye inn, which had its garden just over the high brick
wall of the garden of Lamb House, G. K. Chesterton was staying.
William James had corresponded with our vast contemporary and
he sorely wanted to see him. So with a scandalous directness he
had put the gardener's ladder against that ripe red wall and
clambered up and peeped over!

"Henry had caught him at it.

"It was the sort of thing that isn't done. It was most emphatically
the sort of thing that isn't done. . . . Henry had instructed the
gardener to put away that ladder and William was looking thoroughly naughty about it.

"To Henry's manifest relief, I carried William off and in the road
just outside the town we ran against the Chestertons who had been
for a drive in Romney Marsh; Chesterton was heated and I think
rather swollen by the sunshine; he seemed to overhang his one-
horse fly; he descended slowly but firmly; he was moist and steamy
but cordial; we chatted in the road for a time and William got his
coveted impression."

Pardon this intensely domestic plea. There is nothing I
should like better or enjoy more intensely than to come
over to you for a couple of nights at a less complicated
time. I promise to signal you, appealingly, somewhat
later in the season—before the good days are over. Please
believe in all my embarrassment and regret for this actual
showing meanwhile. Plead for me with H.G., please—
as to my horrid impracticability, tell him I really love him,
and am subject to his potent spell, none the less. My
brother and niece came back to me glowing with a like
affection for you both. Yours dear Mrs. Wells all ruefully yet hopefully and constantly

HENRY JAMES

44

MRS. WHARTON AND HENRY JAMES TO
H. G. AND MRS. WELLS

Spade House, Sandgate
[*November* 1908]

Dear Mrs. Wells (in whom I include H.G.) Mrs.
Wharton (of the "House of Mirth" etc.) has kindly
motored me over from Rye, where she is spending 3 or 4
days with me—but we feel frustrate and dejected and
have only been able to console ourselves by taking
liberties—such as making free with garden and view and

with the beautifullest little boy we have ever seen. We
will come back some other time, when and if we can, and
we are yours both and both most faithfully

HENRY JAMES
EDITH WHARTON

45

JAMES TO MRS. WELLS

Lamb House, Rye, Sussex
Nov. 19, [1908]

DEAR MRS. WELLS.

Mrs. Wharton, staying with me briefly, had motored
me over to Dover to see—and take—a friend (who had
also been with me) off to Paris, and on our way back we
just tried you on the chance—hoping yet a little fearing.
I rejoice that your kind note gives me occasion to explain
that, with a more premeditated visit, we should have in-
fallibly made sure beforehand that you were at home and
that you gave us benevolent leave. Your letter itself is
now *all* benevolence—but Mrs. W's chariot of fire
flashed her away on Tuesday a.m., and me with her again
till last night. I will come over to you some day with
joy, but I am just now asking you to kindly let it—the
happy occasion for me—wait a little for further definition
—as the summer and all the autumn have left my professional integrity shattered by a serious [series] of

devastating assaults and I must, before I do anything else new whatever laboriously piece it together again. Yours and Wells's more than faithfully

HENRY JAMES.

46

JAMES TO WELLS

Lamb House, Rye, Sussex.
October 14th, 1909.

MY DEAR WELLS,

I took down *Ann Veronica*[1] in deep rich draughts during the two days following your magnanimous "donation" of her, and yet have waited till now to vibrate to you visibly and audibly under that pressed spring. I never vibrated under anything of yours, on the whole, I think, *more* than during that intense inglutition; but if I have been hanging fire of acclamation and comment, as I hung it, to my complete self stultification and beyond recovery, over *Tono-Bungay*,[2] it is simply because, confound you, there is so much too much to say, *always*, after every thing of yours; and the critical principle so rages within me (by which I mean the appreciative, the *real* gustatory,) that I tend to labour under the superstition that one must always say *all*. But I can't do that, and I won't—so that I almost intelligently and

[1] Published in October 1909.   [2] Published in February 1909.

coherently choose, which simplifies a little the question. And nothing matters after the fact that you are to me so much the most interesting representational and ironic genius and faculty, of our Anglo-Saxon world and life, in these bemuddled days, that you stand out intensely vivid and alone, making nobody else signify at all. And this has never been more the case than in A.V., where your force and life and ferocious sensibility and heroic cheek all take effect in an extraordinary wealth and truth and beauty and *fury* of impressionism. The quantity of things *done*, in your whole picture, excites my liveliest admiration—so much so that I was able to let myself go, responsively and assentingly, under the strength of the feeling communicated and the impetus accepted, almost as much as if your "method," and fifty other things—by which I mean sharp questions coming up—left me *only* passive and convinced, unchallenging and uninquiring (which they *don't*—no, they don't!) I don't think, as regards this latter point, that I even make out what your subject or Idea, the prime determinant one, may be detected as having *been* (lucidity and logic, on that score, not, to my sense, reigning supreme.) But there I am as if I were wanting to say "all!"—which I'm not now, I find a bit. I only want to say that the thing is irresistible (and indescribable) in its subjective assurance and its rare objective vividness and colour. You must at moments make dear old Dickens turn—for envy of the eye and the ear and the nose and the mouth of you—in his grave. I

don't think the girl herself—her projected Ego—the best
thing in the book—I think it rather wants clearness and
nuances. But the *men* are prodigious, all, and the total
result lives and kicks and throbs and flushes and glares—
I mean hangs there in the very air we breathe; and that
you are a very swagger performer indeed and that I am
your very gaping and grateful
                                                    HENRY JAMES

47

JAMES TO MRS. WELLS

Lamb House, Rye, Sussex.
December 14th, 1909.

DEAR MRS. WELLS.

So kind is your note that I quite blush to be—to *have*
to be—dismally irresponsive. I returned from town
three or four days ago, under urgency, and here for many
weeks to come I am obliged to abide without an absence.
The 20th and 22d alike glitter at me with a vain seduction.
I am very sorry—"social relations" with London (the
whole question of them) are, on this footing of a tempting
nearness and a fatal farness, an endless discipline and
torment. But you and Wells *know*—only now you
laugh and caper; while I pull a longer face than ever and
am yours both very ruefully and, as it were (for having to
stick fast,) gluefully
                                                    HENRY JAMES

48

WELLS TO JAMES

17, *Church Row, Hampstead.*

[*Aug.* 31, 1910]

MY DEAR JAMES.

I've heard of your brother's death [1] with a sense of enormous personal loss. As you know I've seen very little of him but he's been something big and reassuring in my background for many years and what I saw of him at Rye and Sandgate gave me a very living affection for him. I can imagine something of what his death must be to you. I'm filled with impotent concern for you. That all this great edifice of ripened understandings and charities and lucidities should be swept out of the world leaves me baffled and helplessly distressed.

Yours very sincerely

H. G. WELLS

[1] William James died at Chocorua, New Hampshire, 26 August 1910, on returning to America from Europe where he had gone in search of health. Henry James had accompanied his brother and was with him during his last illness.

49

JAMES TO WELLS

Chocorua, N.H.
Sept. 11*th*, 1910.

MY DEAR WELLS.

We greatly value, my sister-in-law and I, your beautiful and tender letter about my beloved Brother and our irreparable loss. Be very gratefully thanked for it, and know we are deeply moved by your admirably-expressed sense of what he *was*, so nobly and magnanimously. He did surely shed light to man, and *gave*, of his own great spirit and beautiful genius, with splendid generosity. Of my personal loss—the extinction of so shining a presence in my own life, and from so far back (really from dimmest childhood) I won't pretend to speak. He had an inexhaustible authority for me, and I feel abandoned and afraid, even as a lost child. But he is a possession, of real magnitude, and I shall find myself still living upon him to the end. My life, thank God, is impregnated with him. My sister-in-law and his children are very interesting and absorbing to me, and I shall stay on here (in America I mean) for some months—so that we may hold and cling together. And I hope in the future never to be without some of them. When I return to England I shall see you promptly—and you have perhaps meanwhile an inadequate idea of the moral and aesthetic greed (enriched by criticism) with which I read you. Yours all faithfully

HENRY JAMES

50

JAMES TO WELLS

95 *Irving Street,*
Cambridge, Mass.
March 3rd, 1911.

MY DEAR WELLS.

I seem to have had notice from my housekeeper at Rye that you have very kindly sent me there a copy of the *New Machiavelli* [1]—which she has forborne to forward me to these Tariff-guarded shores; in obedience to my general instructions. But this needn't prevent me from thanking you for the generous gift, which will keep company with a brave row of other such valued signs of your remembrance at Lamb House: thanking you all the more too that I hadn't waited for gift or guerdon to fall on you and devour you, but have just lately been finding the American issue of your wondrous book a sufficient occasion for that. Thus it is that I can't rest longer till I make you some small sign at last of my conscious indebtedness.

I have read you then, I need scarcely tell you, with an intensified sense of that life and force and temperament,

[1] Published in January 1911.

that fulness of endowment and easy impudence of genius, which make you so extraordinary and which have long claimed my unstinted admiration; you being for me so much the most interesting and masterful prose-painter of your English generation (or indeed of your generation unqualified,) that I see you hang there over the subject scene practically all alone; a far-flaring even though turbid and smoky lamp, projecting the most vivid and splendid golden splotches, *creating* them about the field—shining scattered innumerable morsels of a huge smashed mirror. I seem to feel that there can be no better proof of your great gift—*The N.M.* makes me most particularly feel it—than that you bedevil and coerce to the extent you do such a reader and victim as I am; I mean one so engaged on the side of ways and attempts to which yours are extremely alien and for whom the great interest of the art we practice involves a lot of considerations and pre-occupations over which you more and more ride rough-shod and triumphant—when you don't, that is, with a strange and brilliant impunity of your own, leave them to one side altogether (which *is* indeed what you now apparently incline most to do.) Your big feeling for life, your capacity for chewing up the thickness of the world in such enormous mouthfuls, while you fairly slobber, so to speak, with the multitudinous taste—this constitutes for me a rare and wonderful and admirable exhibition, on your part, in itself, so that one should doubtless frankly ask one's self what the devil, in the way

of effect and evocation and general demonic activity, one
wants more. Well, I am willing for today to let it stand
at that; the whole of the earlier part of the book, or the first
half, is so alive and kicking and sprawling!—so vivid
and rich and strong—above all so *amusing* (in the high
sense of the word;) and I make my remonstrance—for I
do remonstrate—bear upon the bad service you have
done your cause by riding so hard again that accurst autobiographic form which puts a premium on the loose, the
improvised, the cheap and the easy.[1] Save in the fantastic and the romantic (Copperfield, Jane Eyre, that
charming thing of Stevenson's with the bad title—"Kid-
napped"?) it has no authority, no persuasive or convincing force—its grasp of reality and truth isn't strong
and disinterested. R. Crusoe, e.g., isn't a novel at all.
There is, to my vision, no authentic, and no really
interesting and no *beautiful*, report of things on the
novelist's, the painter's part unless a particular detachment has operated, unless the great stewpot or crucible
of the imagination, of the observant and recording and
interpreting mind in short, has intervened and played its
part—and this detachment, this chemical transmutation

---

[1] James here is echoing a view he held from his earliest writing
years: that the novelist should use the first person for a long
narrative only under special circumstances. The question is dealt
with at some length in his preface to *The Ambassadors*, where he
describes the first person in the long novel as "the dark abyss of
romance" which foredooms it to "looseness . . . The terrible
fluidity of self-revelation."

for the aesthetic, the representational, end is terribly
wanting in autobiography brought, as the horrible
phrase is, up to date. That's my main "criticism" on *The
N.M.*—and on the whole ground there would be a
hundred things more to say. It's accurst that I am not
near enough to you to say them in less floundering
fashion than this—but give me time (I return to England
in June, never again, D.V., to leave it—surprise Mr.
Remington thereby as I may!) [1] and we will jaw as far as
you will keep me company. Meanwhile I don't *want* to
send across the wintry sea anything but my expressed
gratitude for the immense impressionistic and speculative
wealth and variety of your book. Yours, my dear Wells,
ever,   HENRY JAMES

P.S. I think the exhibition of "Love" *as* "Love"—
functional Love—always suffers from a certain inevitable
and insurmountable flat-footedness (for the reader's
nerves etc.;) which is only to be counterplotted by round-
about arts—as by tracing it through indirectness and tor-
tuosities of application and effect—to keep it somehow
interesting and productive (though I don't mean *re*productive!) But this again is a big subject.

*P.S.*2. I am like your hero's forsaken wife: I know
having things (the things of life, history, the world,) only
as, and by *keeping* them. So, and so only, I *do* have them!

---

[1] In *The New Machiavelli* Richard Remington relates the story
of his life from the Ligurian coast where he is in voluntary exile
from England.

I

51

WELLS TO JAMES

17, *Church Row, Hampstead.*
[*April* 25, 1911],

MY DEAR JAMES.

I've been putting off answering your letter because I
wanted to answer it properly and here at last comes the
meagre apology for a response to the most illuminating
of comments. So far as it is loving chastisement I think
I wholly agree and kiss the rod. You put your sense
of the turbid confusion, the strain and violence of my
book so beautifully that almost they seem merits. But
oh! some day when I'm settled-er if ever, I will do
better. I agree about the 'first-person'. The only artistic
'first-person' is the onlooker speculative 'first person',
and God helping me, this shall be the last of my gush-
ing Hari-Karis. But the guts and guts and guts and
guts I've poured out all over the blessed libraries and
J. A. Spender [1] and everybody! I run against all sorts
of people festooned with the apparently unlimited
stuff. . . .

No!—It shall be the end of it.

I wish you were over here. I rarely go to the Reform
without a strange wild hope of seeing you. In June I am

---

[1] John Alfred Spender, editor of the *Westminster Gazette.*

going with all my household to a home in France and I
shall return to London in October. Thenabouts perhaps
you'll be out.

Very sincerely yours

H. G. WELLS

52

H. G. WELLS

"The Contemporary Novel" [1]

CIRCUMSTANCES have made me think a good deal at
different times about the business of writing novels, and
what it means, and is, and may be; and I was a professional critic of novels long before I wrote them. I
have been writing novels, or writing about novels, for
the last twenty years. It seems only yesterday that I
wrote a review—the first long and appreciative review he
had—of Mr. Joseph Conrad's "Almayer's Folly" in the
Saturday Review. When a man has focussed so much of
his life upon the novel, it is not reasonable to expect him
to take too modest or apologetic a view of it. I consider
the novel an important and necessary thing indeed in that
complicated system of uneasy adjustments and readjust-
ments which is modern civilisation. I make very high

---

[1] *An Englishman Looks at the World* (London, 1914), pp. 148–
69, the first book appearance of the talk given to the Times Book
Club in 1911 on "The Scope of the Novel." For both serial and
book publication Wells re-titled the paper, which he revised,
"The Contemporary Novel."

and wide claims for it. In many directions I do not think we can get along without it.

Now this, I know, is not the usually received opinion. There is, I am aware, the theory that the novel is wholly and solely a means of relaxation. In spite of manifest facts, that was the dominant view of the great period that we now in our retrospective way speak of as the Victorian, and it still survives to this day. It is the man's theory of the novel rather than the woman's. One may call it the Weary Giant theory. The reader is represented as a man, burthened, toiling, worn. He has been in his office from ten to four, with perhaps only two hours' interval at his club for lunch; or he has been playing golf; or he has been waiting about and voting in the House; or he has been fishing; or he has been disputing a point of law; or writing a sermon; or doing one of a thousand other of the grave important things which constitute the substance of a prosperous man's life. Now at last comes the little precious interval of leisure, and the Weary Giant takes up a book. Perhaps he is vexed: he may have been bunkered, his line may have been entangled in the trees, his favourite investment may have slumped, or the judge have had indignation and been extremely rude to him. He wants to forget the troublesome realities of life. He wants to be taken out of himself, to be cheered, consoled, amused—above all, amused. He doesn't want ideas, he doesn't want facts; above all, he doesn't want— *Problems*. He wants to dream of the bright, thin, gay

excitements of a phantom world—in which he can be
hero—of horses ridden and lace worn and princesses
rescued and won. He wants pictures of funny slums, and
entertaining paupers, and laughable longshoremen, and
kindly impulses making life sweet. He wants romance
without its defiance, and humour without its sting; and
the business of the novelist, he holds, is to supply this
cooling refreshment. That is the Weary Giant theory of
the novel. It ruled British criticism up to the period of
the Boer war—and then something happened to quite a
lot of us, and it has never completely recovered its old
predominance. Perhaps it will; perhaps something else
may happen to prevent its ever doing so.

Both fiction and criticism to-day are in revolt against
that tired giant, the prosperous Englishman. I cannot
think of a single writer of any distinction to-day, unless
it is Mr. W. W. Jacobs, who is content merely to serve
the purpose of those slippered hours. So far from the
weary reader being a decently tired giant, we realise that
he is only an inexpressibly lax, slovenly and undertrained
giant, and we are all out with one accord resolved to
exercise his higher ganglia in every possible way. And
so I will say no more of the idea that the novel is merely a
harmless opiate for the vacant hours of prosperous men.
As a matter of fact, it never has been, and by its nature I
doubt if it ever can be.

I do not think that women have ever quite succumbed
to the tired giant attitude in their reading. Women are

more serious, not only about life, but about books. No type or kind of woman is capable of that lounging, defensive stupidity which is the basis of the tired giant attitude, and all through the early 'nineties, during which the respectable frivolity of Great Britain left its most enduring marks upon our literature, there was a rebel undertow of earnest and aggressive writing and reading, supported chiefly by women and supplied very largely by women, which gave the lie to the prevailing trivial estimate of fiction. Among readers, women and girls and young men at least will insist upon having their novels significant and real, and it is to these perpetually renewed elements in the public that the novelist must look for his continuing emancipation from the wearier and more massive influences at work in contemporary British life.

And if the novel is to be recognised as something more than a relaxation, it has also, I think, to be kept free from the restrictions imposed upon it by the fierce pedantries of those who would define a general form for it. Every art nowadays must steer its way between the rocks of trivial and degrading standards and the whirlpool of arbitrary and irrational criticism. Whenever criticism of any art becomes specialised and professional, whenever a class of adjudicators is brought into existence, those adjudicators are apt to become as a class distrustful of their immediate impressions, and anxious for methods of comparison between work and work, they begin to emulate the classifications and exact measurements of a science, and

to set up ideals and rules as data for such classi-
fication and measurements. They develop an alleged
sense of technique, which is too often no more than
the attempt to exact a laboriousness of method, or to
insist upon peculiarities of method which impress the
professional critic not so much as being merits as being
meritorious. This sort of thing has gone very far with the
critical discussion both of the novel and the play. You
have all heard that impressive dictum that some particular theatrical display, although moving, interesting,
and continually entertaining from start to finish, was for
occult technical reasons "not a play," and in the same way
you are continually having your appreciation of fiction
dashed by the mysterious parallel condemnation, that the
story you like "isn't a novel." The novel has been
treated as though its form was as well-defined as the
sonnet. Some year or so ago, for example, there was a
quite serious discussion, which began, I believe, in a
weekly paper devoted to the interests of various noncon-
formist religious organisations, about the proper length
for a novel. The critic was to begin his painful duties
with a yard measure. The matter was taken up with profound gravity by the *Westminster Gazette*, and a considerable number of literary men and women were cir-
cularised and asked to state, in the face of "Tom Jones,"
"The Vicar of Wakefield," "The Shabby-Genteel Story,"
and "Bleak House," just exactly how long the novel ought
to be. Our replies varied according to the civility of our

natures, but the mere attempt to raise the question shows, I think, how widespread among the editorial, paragraph-writing, opinion-making sort of people is this notion of prescribing a definite length and a definite form for the novel. In the newspaper correspondence that followed, our friend the weary giant made a transitory appearance again. We were told the novel ought to be long enough for him to take up after dinner and finish before his whisky at eleven.

That was obviously a half-forgotten echo of Edgar Allan Poe's discusssion of the short story. Edgar Allan Poe was very definite upon the point that the short story should be finished at a sitting. But the novel and short story are two entirely different things, and the train of reasoning that made the American master limit the short story to about an hour of reading as a maximum, does not apply to the longer work. A short story is, or should be, a simple thing; it aims at producing one single, vivid effect; it has to seize the attention at the outset, and never relaxing, gather it together more and more until the climax is reached. The limits of the human capacity to attend closely therefore set a limit to it; it must explode and finish before interruption occurs or fatigue sets in. But the novel I hold to be a discursive thing; it is not a single interest, but a woven tapestry of interests; one is drawn on first by this affection and curiosity, and then by that; it is something to return to, and I do not see that we can possibly set any limit to its extent. The distinctive

value of the novel among written works of art is in
characterisation, and the charm of a well-conceived
character lies, not in knowing its destiny, but in watching
its proceedings. For my own part, I will confess that I
find all the novels of Dickens, long as they are, too short
for me. I am sorry they do not flow into one another
more than they do. I wish Micawber and Dick Swiveller
and Sairey Gamp turned up again in other novels than
their own, just as Shakespeare ran the glorious glow of
Falstaff through a group of plays. But Dickens tried this
once when he carried on the Pickwick Club into "Master
Humphrey's Clock." That experiment was unsatisfactory, and he did not attempt anything of the sort
again. Following on the days of Dickens, the novel began to contract, to subordinate characterisation to story
and description to drama; considerations of a sordid
nature, I am told, had to do with that; something about a
guinea and a half and six shillings with which we will
not concern ourselves [1]—but I rejoice to see many signs
to-day that that phase of narrowing and restriction is
over, and that there is every encouragement for a return
towards a laxer, more spacious form of novel-writing.
The movement is partly of English origin, a revolt against
those more exacting and cramping conceptions of artistic
perfection to which I will recur in a moment, and a re-

---

[1] During the eighteen-eighties and eighteen-nineties, the three-
volume novel at thirty-one shillings and sixpence gradually gave
way to the one-volume novel at six shillings.

turn to the lax freedom of form, the rambling discursiveness, the right to roam, of the earlier English novel, of "Tristram Shandy" and of "Tom Jones"; and partly it comes from abroad, and derives a stimulus from such bold and original enterprises as that of Monsieur Rolland in his "Jean Christophe." Its double origin involves a double nature; for while the English spirit is towards discursiveness and variety, the new French movement is rather towards exhaustiveness. Mr. Arnold Bennett has experimented in both forms of amplitude. His superb "Old Wives' Tale," wandering from person to person and from scene to scene, is by far the finest "long novel" that has been written in English in the English fashion in this generation, and now in "Clayhanger" and its promised collaterals,[1] he undertakes that complete, minute, abundant presentation of the growth and modification of one or two individual minds, which is the essential characteristic of the Continental movement towards the novel of amplitude. While the "Old Wives' Tale" is discursive, "Clayhanger" is exhaustive; he gives us both types of the new movement in perfection.

I name "Jean Christophe" as a sort of archetype in this connection, because it is just at present very much in our thoughts by reason of the admirable translation Mr. Cannan is giving us; but there is a greater predecessor to

[1] Bennett published *Hilda Lessways* and *These Twain*, the remaining volumes of the *Clayhanger* trilogy, in 1911 and 1916 respectively.

this comprehensive and spectacular treatment of a single mind and its impressions and ideas, or of one or two associated minds, that comes to us now *via* Mr. Bennett and Mr. Cannan from France. The great original of all this work is that colossal last unfinished book of Flaubert, "Bouvard et Pécuchet." Flaubert, the bulk of whose life was spent upon the most austere and restrained fiction— Turgenev was not more austere and restrained—broke out at last into this gay, sad miracle of intellectual abundance. It is not extensively read in this country; it is not yet, I believe, translated into English; but there it is— and if it is new to the reader I make him this present of the secret of a book that is a precious wilderness of wonderful reading. But if Flaubert is really the Continental emancipator of the novel from the restrictions of form, the master to whom we of the English persuasion, we of the discursive school, must for ever recur is he, whom I will maintain against all comers to be the subtlest and greatest *artist*—I lay stress upon that word artist—that Great Britain has ever produced in all that is essentially the novel, Laurence Sterne. . . .

The confusion between the standards of a short story and the standards of the novel which leads at last to these —what shall I call them?—*Westminster Gazettisms?*— about the correct length to which the novelist should aspire, leads also to all kinds of absurd condemnations and exactions upon matters of method and style. The underlying fallacy is always this: the assumption that the novel, like the story, aims at a single, concentrated impression. From that comes a fertile growth of error. Constantly one finds in the reviews of works of fiction the complaint that this, that or the other thing in a novel is irrelevant. Now it is the easiest thing, and most fatal thing, to become irrelevant in a short story. A short story should go to its point as a man flies from a pursuing tiger: he pauses not for the daisies in his path, or to note the pretty moss on the tree he climbs for safety. But the novel by comparison is like breakfasting in the open air on a summer morning; nothing is irrelevant if the writer's mood is happy, and the tapping of the thrush upon the garden path, or the petal of apple-blossom that floats down into my coffee, is as relevant as the egg I open or the bread and butter I bite. And all sorts of things that inevitably mar the tense illusion which is the aim of the short story—the introduction, for example, of the author's personality—any comment that seems to admit that, after all, fiction is fiction, a change in manner between part and part, burlesque, parody, invective, all such things are not necessarily wrong in the novel. Of course, all these things may fail in their effect; they may jar, hinder, irritate, and all are difficult to do well; but it is no artistic merit to evade a difficulty any more than it is a merit in a hunter to refuse even the highest of fences. Nearly all the novels that have, by the lapse of time, reached an assured position of recognised greatness, are not only saturated in the personality of the author, but have in addition quite unaffected personal outbreaks. The least successful instance, the one that is made the text against all such first-personal interventions, is, of course, Thackeray. But I think the trouble with Thackeray is not that he makes first-personal interventions, but that he does so with a curious touch of dishonesty. I agree with the late Mrs. Craigie that there was something profoundly vulgar about Thackeray. It was a sham thoughtful, sham man-of-the-world pose he assumed; it is an aggressive, conscious, challenging person astride before a fire, and a little distended by dinner and a sense of social and literary precedences, who uses the first person in Thackeray's novels. It isn't the real Thackeray; it isn't a frank man who looks you in the eyes and bares his soul and demands your sympathy. That is a criticism of Thackeray, but it isn't a condemnation of intervention.

I admit that for a movelist to come in person in this way before his readers involves grave risks; but when it is done without affectations, starkly as a man comes in out of the darkness to tell of perplexing things without—as, for instance, Mr. Joseph Conrad does for all practical purposes in his "Lord Jim"—then it gives a sort of depth, a sort of subjective reality, that no such cold, almost affectedly ironical detachment as that which distinguishes the work of Mr. John Galsworthy, for example, can ever attain. And in some cases the whole art and delight of a novel may lie in the author's personal interventions; let such novels as "Elizabeth and her German Garden," and the same writer's "Elizabeth in Rügen,"[1] bear witness.

Now, all this time I have been hacking away at certain hampering and limiting beliefs about the novel, letting it loose, as it were, in form and purpose; I have still to say just what I think the novel is, and where, if anywhere, its boundary-line ought to be drawn. It is by no means an easy task to define the novel. It is not a thing premeditated. It is a thing that has grown up into modern life, and taken upon itself uses and produced results that could not have been foreseen by its originators. Few of the important things in the collective life of man started out to be what they are. Consider, for example, all the unexpected aesthetic values, the inspiration and variety of emotional result which arises out of the cross-shaped plan of the Gothic cathedral, and the undesigned delight and wonder of white marble that has ensued, as I have been told, through the ageing and whitening of the realistically coloured statuary of the Greeks and Romans. Much of the charm of the old furniture and needlework, again, upon which the present time sets so much store, lies in acquired and unpremeditated qualities. And no doubt the novel grew up out of simple story-telling, and the universal desire of children, old and young alike, for a story. It is only slowly that we have developed the distinction of the novel from the romance, as being a story

[1] By Wells's friend, the Countess von Arnim, later Countess Russell.

of human beings, absolutely credible and conceivable, as distinguished from human beings frankly endowed with the glamour, the wonder, the brightness, of a less exacting and more vividly eventful world. The novel is a story that demands, or professes to demand, no make-believe. The novelist undertakes to present you people and things as real as any that you can meet in an omnibus. And I suppose it is conceivable that a novel might exist which was just purely a story of that kind and nothing more. It might amuse you as one is amused by looking out of a window into a street, or listening to a piece of agreeable music, and that might be the limit of its effect. But almost always the novel is something more than that, and produces more effect than that. The novel has inseparable moral consequences. It leaves impressions, not simply of things seen, but of acts judged and made attractive or unattractive. They may prove very slight moral consequences, and very shallow moral impressions in the long run, but there they are, none the less, its inevitable accompaniments. It is unavoidable that this should be so. Even if the novelist attempts or affects to be impartial, he still cannot prevent his characters setting examples; he still cannot avoid, as people say, putting ideas into his readers' heads. The greater his skill, the more convincing his treatment, the more vivid his power of suggestion. And it is equally impossible for him not to betray his sense that the proceedings of this person are rather jolly and admirable, and of that, rather ugly and detestable.

I suppose Mr. Bennett, for example, would say that he should not do so; but it is as manifest to any disinterested observer that he greatly loves and admires his Card, as that Richardson admired his Sir Charles Grandison, or that Mrs. Humphry Ward considers her Marcella a very fine and estimable young woman. And I think it is just in this, that the novel is not simply a fictitious record of conduct, but also a study and judgement of conduct, and through that of the ideas that lead to conduct, that the real and increasing value—or perhaps to avoid controversy I had better say the real and increasing importance—of the novel and of the novelist in modern life comes in.

It is no new discovery that the novel, like the drama, is a powerful instrument of moral suggestion. This has been understood in England ever since there has been such a thing as a novel in England. This has been recognised equally by novelists, novel-readers, and the people who wouldn't read novels under any condition whatever. Richardson wrote deliberately for edification, and "Tom Jones" is a powerful and effective appeal for a charitable, and even indulgent, attitude towards loose-living men. But excepting Fielding and one or two other of those partial exceptions that always occur in the case of critical generalisations, there is a definable difference between the novel of the past and what I may call the modern novel. It is a difference that is reflected upon the novel from a difference in the general way of thinking. It lies in the fact that formerly there was a feeling of certitude about moral values and standards of conduct that is altogether absent to-day. It wasn't so much that men were agreed upon these things—about these things there have always been enormous divergences of opinion—as that men were emphatic, cocksure, and unteachable about whatever they did happen to believe to a degree that no longer obtains. This is the Balfourian age, and even religion seeks to establish itself on doubt. There were, perhaps, just as many differences in the past as there are now, but the outlines were harder—they were, indeed, so hard as to be almost, to our sense, savage. You might be a Roman Catholic, and in that case you did not want to hear about Protestants, Turks, Infidels, except in tones of horror and hatred. You knew exactly what was good and what was evil. Your priest informed you upon these points, and all you needed in any novel you read was a confirmation, implicit or explicit, of these vivid, rather than charming, prejudices. If you were a Protestant you were equally clear and unshakable. Your sect, whichever sect you belonged to, knew the whole of truth and included all the nice people. It had nothing to learn in the world, and it wanted to learn nothing outside its sectarian convictions. The unbelievers, you know, were just as bad, and said their creeds with an equal fury —merely interpolating *nots*. People of every sort— Catholic, Protestant, Infidel, or what not—were equally clear that good was good and bad was bad, that the world

K

was made up of good characters whom you had to love, help and admire, and of bad characters to whom one might, in the interests of goodness, even lie, and whom one had to foil, defeat and triumph over shamelessly at every opportunity. That was the quality of the times. The novel reflected this quality of assurance, and its utmost charity was to unmask an apparent villain and show that he or she was really profoundly and correctly good, or to unmask an apparent saint and show the hypocrite. There was no such penetrating and pervading element of doubt and curiosity—and charity, about the rightfulness and beauty of conduct, such as one meets on every hand to-day.

The novel-reader of the past, therefore, like the novel-reader of the more provincial parts of England to-day, judged a novel by the convictions that had been built up in him by his training and his priest or his pastor. If it agreed with these convictions he approved; if it did not agree he disapproved—often with great energy. The novel, where it was not unconditionally banned altogether as a thing disturbing and unnecessary, was regarded as a thing subordinated to the teaching of the priest or pastor, or whatever director and dogma was followed. Its modest moral confirmations began when authority had completed its direction. The novel was good—if it seemed to harmonise with the graver exercises conducted by Mr. Chadband—and it was bad and outcast if Mr. Chadband said so. And it is over the bodies of

discredited and disgruntled Chadbands that the novel
escapes from its servitude and inferiority.

Now the conflict of authority against criticism is one
of the eternal conflicts of humanity. It is the conflict
of organisation against initiative, of discipline against
freedom. It was the conflict of the priest against the
prophet in ancient Judæa, of the Pharisee against the
Nazarene, of the Realist against the Nominalist, of the
Church against the Franciscan and the Lollard, of the
Respectable Person against the Artist, of the hedge-
clippers of mankind against the shooting buds. And
to-day, while we live in a period of tightening and ex-
tending social organisation, we live also in a period of
adventurous and insurgent thought, in an intellectual
spring unprecedented in the world's history. There is an
enormous criticism going on of the faiths upon which
men's lives and associations are based, and of every
standard and rule of conduct. And it is inevitable that
the novel, just in the measure of its sincerity and ability,
should reflect and co-operate in the atmosphere and un-
certainties and changing variety of this seething and
creative time.

And I do not mean merely that the novel is unavoid-
ably charged with the representation of this wide and
wonderful conflict. It is a necessary part of the conflict.
The essential characteristic of this great intellectual
revolution amidst which we are living to-day, that revolution of which the revival and restatement of nominalism

under the name of pragmatism is the philosophical aspect, consists in the reassertion of the importance of the individual instance as against the generalisation. All our social, political, moral problems are being approached in a new spirit, in an inquiring and experimental spirit, which has small respect for abstract principles and deductive rules. We perceive more and more clearly, for example, that the study of social organisation is an empty and unprofitable study until we approach it as a study of the association and inter-reaction of individualised human beings inspired by diversified motives, ruled by traditions, and swayed by the suggestions of a complex intellectual atmosphere. And all our conceptions of the relationships between man and man, and of justice and rightfulness and social desirableness, remain something misfitting and inappropriate, something uncomfortable and potentially injurious, as if we were trying to wear sharp-edged clothes made for a giant out of tin, until we bring them to the test and measure of realised individualities.

And this is where the value and opportunity of the modern novel comes in. So far as I can see, it is the only medium through which we can discuss the great majority of the problems which are being raised in such bristling multitude by our contemporary social development. Nearly every one of those problems has at its core a psychological problem, and not merely a psychological problem, but one in which the idea of individuality is an essential factor. Dealing with most of these questions by a rule or a generalisation is like putting a cordon round a jungle full of the most diversified sort of game. The hunting only begins when you leave the cordon behind you and push into the thickets.

Take, for example, the immense cluster of difficulties that arises out of the increasing complexity of our state. On every hand we are creating officials, and compared with only a few years ago the private life in a dozen fresh directions comes into contact with officialdom. But we still do practically nothing to work out the interesting changes that occur in this sort of man and that, when you withdraw him as it were from the common crowd of humanity, put his mind if not his body into uniform and endow him with powers and functions and rules. It is manifestly a study of the profoundest public and personal importance. It is manifestly a study of increasing importance. The process of social and political organisation that has been going on for the last quarter of a century is pretty clearly going on now if anything with increasing vigour—and for the most part the entire dependence of the consequences of the whole problem upon the reaction between the office on the one hand and the weak, uncertain, various human beings who take office on the other, doesn't seem even to be suspected by the energetic, virtuous and more or less amiable people whose activities in politics and upon the backstairs of politics bring about these developments. They assume that the sort of official they need, a combination of god-like virtue and intelligence with unfailing mechanical obedience, can be made out of just any young nephew. And I know of no means of persuading people that this is a rather unjustifiable assumption, and of creating an intelligent controlling criticism of officials and of assisting conscientious officials to an effective self-examination, and generally of keeping the atmosphere of official life sweet and healthy, except the novel. Yet so far the novel has scarcely begun its attack upon this particular field of human life, and all the attractive varied play of motive it contains.

Of course we have one supreme and devastating study of the illiterate minor official in Bumble. That one figure lit up and still lights the whole problem of Poor Law administration for the English reading community. It was a translation of well-meant regulations and pseudo-scientific conceptions of social order into blundering, arrogant, ill-bred flesh and blood. It was worth a hundred Royal Commissions. You may make your regulations as you please, said Dickens in effect; this is one sample of the stuff that will carry them out. But Bumble stands almost alone. Instead of realising that he is only one aspect of officialdom, we are all too apt to make him the type of all officials, and not an urban district council can get into a dispute about its electric light without being denounced as a Bumbledom by some whirling enemy or other. The burthen upon Bumble's shoulders is too heavy to be borne, and we want the contemporary novel to give us a score of other figures to put beside him, other aspects and reflections upon this great problem of officialism made flesh. Bumble is a magnificent figure of the follies and cruelties of ignorance in office—I would have every candidate for the post of workhouse master pass a severe examination upon "Oliver Twist"—but it is not only caricature and satire I demand. We must have not only the fullest treatment of the temptations, vanities, abuses, and absurdities of office, but all its dreams, its sense of constructive order, its consolations, its sense of service, and its nobler satisfactions. You may say that is demanding more insight and power in our novels and novelists than we can possibly hope to find in them. So much the worse for us. I stick to my thesis that the complicated social organisation of to-day cannot get along without the amount of mutual understanding and mutual explanation such a range of characterisation in our novels implies. The success of civilisation amounts ultimately to a success of sympathy and understanding. If people cannot be brought to an interest in one another greater than they feel to-day, to curiosities and criticisms far keener, and co-operations far subtler than we have now; if class cannot be brought to measure itself against, and interchange experience and sympathy with class, and temperament with temperament, then we shall never struggle very far beyond the confused discomforts and uneasiness of to-day, and the changes and complications of human life will remain as they are now, very like the crumplings and separations and complications of an immense avalanche that is sliding down a hill. And in this tremendous work of human reconciliation and elucidation, it seems to me it is the novel that must attempt most and achieve most.

You may feel disposed to say to all this: We grant the major premises, but why look to the work of prose fiction as the main instrument in this necessary process of, so to speak, sympathising humanity together? Cannot this be done far more effectively through biography and autobiography, for example? Isn't there the lyric; and, above all, isn't there the play? Well, so far as the stage goes, I think it is a very charming and exciting form of human activity, a display of actions and surprises of the most moving and impressive sort; but beyond the opportunity it affords for saying startling and thought-provoking things—opportunities Mr. Shaw, for example, has worked to the utmost limit—I do not see that the drama does much to enlarge our sympathies and add to our stock of motive ideas. And regarded as a medium for startling and thought-provoking things, the stage seems to me an extremely clumsy and costly affair. One might just as well go about with a pencil writing up the thought-provoking phrase, whatever it is, on walls. The drama excites our sympathies intensely, but it seems to me it is far too objective a medium to widen them appreciably, and it is that widening, that increase in the range of understanding, at which I think civilisation is aiming. The case for biography, and more particularly autobiography, as against the novel, is, I admit, at the first blush stronger. You may say: Why give us these creatures of a novelist's imagination, these phantom and fantastic thinkings and doings, when we may have the stories of real lives, really lived—the intimate record of actual men and women? To which one answers: "Ah, if one could! But it is just because biography does deal with actual lives, actual facts, because it radiates out to touch continuing interests and sensitive survivors, that it is so unsatisfactory, so untruthful. Its inseparable falsehood is the worst of all kinds of falsehood—the falsehood of omission. Think what an abounding, astonishing, perplexing person Gladstone must have been in life, and consider Lord Morley's "Life of Gladstone," cold, dignified—not a life at all, indeed, so much as embalmed remains; the fire gone, the passions gone, the bowels carefully removed. All biography has something of that post-mortem coldness and respect, and as for autobiography— a man may show his soul in a thousand half-conscious ways, but to turn upon oneself and explain oneself is given to no one. It is the natural liars and braggarts, your Cellinis and Casanovas, men with a habit of regarding themselves with a kind of objective admiration, who do best in autobiography. And, on the other hand, the novel has neither the intense self-consciousness of autobiography nor the paralysing responsibilities of the biographer. It is by comparison irresponsible and free. Because its characters are figments and phantoms, they can be made entirely transparent. Because they are fictions, and you know they are fictions, so that they cannot hold you for an instant so soon as they cease to be true, they have a power of veracity quite beyond that of actual records. Every novel carries its own justification and its own condemnation in its success or failure to convince you that *the thing was so*. Now history, biography, blue-book, and so forth, can hardly ever get beyond the statement that the superficial fact was so.

You see now the scope of the claim I am making for the novel; it is to be the social mediator, the vehicle of understanding, the instrument of self-examination, the parade of morals and the exchange of manners, the factory of customs, the criticism of laws and institutions and of social dogmas and ideas. It is to be the home confessional, the initiator of knowledge, the seed of fruitful self-questioning. Let me be very clear here. I do not mean for a moment that the novelist is going to set up as a teacher, as a sort of priest with a pen, who will make men and women believe and do this and that. The novel is not a new sort of pulpit; humanity is passing out of the phase when men *sit under* preachers and dogmatic influences. But the novelist is going to be the most potent of artists, because he is going to present conduct, devise beautiful conduct, discuss conduct, analyse conduct, suggest conduct, illuminate it through and through. He will not teach, but discuss, point out, plead, and display. And this being my view you will be prepared for the demand I am now about to make for an absolutely free hand for the novelist in his choice of topic and incident and in his method of treatment; or rather, if I may presume to speak for other novelists, I would say it is not so much a demand we make as an intention we proclaim. We are going to write, subject only to our limitations, about the whole of human life. We are going to deal with political questions and religious questions and social questions. We cannot present people unless we have this free hand, this unrestricted field. What is the good of telling stories about people's lives if one may not deal freely with the religious beliefs and organisations that have controlled or failed to control them? What is the good of pretending to write about love, and the loyalties and treacheries and quarrels of men and women, if one must not glance at those varieties of physical temperament and organic quality, those deeply passionate needs and distresses from which half the storms of human life are brewed? We mean to deal with all these things, and it will need very much more than the disapproval of provincial librarians, the hostility of a few influential people in London, the scurrility of one paper,[1] and the deep and obstinate

---

[1] The *Spectator*, owned by J. St Loe Strachey, where a reviewer had written of *Ann Veronica* that "the muddy world of Mr. Wells's imaginings" was "a community of scuffling stoats and ferrets, unenlightened by a ray of duty and abnegation."

silences of another,[1] to stop the incoming tide of aggressive novel-writing. We are going to write about it all. We are going to write about business and finance and politics and precedence and pretentiousness and decorum and indecorum, until a thousand pretences and ten thousand impostures shrivel in the cold, clear air of our elucidations. We are going to write of wasted opportunities and latent beauties until a thousand new ways of living open to men and women. We are going to appeal to the young and the hopeful and the curious, against the established, the dignified, and defensive. Before we have done, we will have all life within the scope of the novel.

53

JAMES TO MRS. WELLS

Reform Club, Pall Mall, S.W.

March 2d, 1912

DEAR MRS. WELLS,

It's a queer time for joyous gambols—but I'm not sure it isn't the *right* time for a fine whistling in the dark. Therefore I'll come on Friday 8th with great pleasure and great hope: hope that it will do us all good.[2] I shall whistle as hard as I can. It is to the *Library*, I assume, we

---

[1] The *Westminster Gazette*.

[2] The occasion was a fancy dress dance at Wells's. James attended, in formal attire, in the company of Hugh Walpole and the Countess von Arnim.

come—but if I am not admitted there without your protection I will come round, to C.R.[1] In fact it will be quite simple to go to C.R. *first* and see, and I am yours all faithfully

HENRY JAMES

54

JAMES TO WELLS

The Reform Club,
March 20th, 1912.

MY DEAR WELLS.

It has been a great sorrow—verily a shock to me—to hear from Edmund Gosse that you are not disposed to avail yourself of our invitation to Membership of the Academic Committee.[2] Is it not possible to you to reconsider—under a fond and passionate appeal—that irresponsive and unsociable attitude? On hearing of your election I felt a greater pleasure than anything in my connection with the body had yet given me, and if you maintain your refusal I shall continue, in pain and privation, to yearn for you. So I am moved to try respectfully to contend with you to some good issue on the subject. Even if you have reasons more substantial than I imagine,

[1] Church Row, Hampstead, where the Wellses lived.
[2] The Academic Committee of the Royal Society of Literature included at this date, among other distinguished members, Barrie, Bridges, Conrad, Galsworthy, Hardy, James, Gilbert Murray, Shaw and Yeats.

or *can* imagine, have them, I mean, as the matter has
hitherto struck you, I find it in me to promise you, as it
were, in the light of my own experience (for I too have
had an experience!) that they won't seem to you *after
the fact*—that is if you only *would* come in!—half as valid
as they do now. The thing is a *pleasant* and a plastic,
elastic, aspiring thing, greatly appealing to our good-will
—by which I especially mean to yours, that of your
literary and creative generation; offering us no rigour,
offering us opportunities for influence, for pressure in
desirable directions and asking no sacrifice worth
speaking of or grudging in return. It will be what the
best of us shall make it, and it is open to the best of us to
make it more interesting and more amusing (if you will—
"in the highest sense of the term") to ourselves, and more
suggestive to others. Above all it would be so fortified
by your accession that a due consideration for the
prestige of current English letters surely ought to move
you. You would do something for us that we lack and
don't want to lack—and we would do for *you*, I think,
that you would find yourself *within* still more moved than
without to that critical, that ironic, that even exasperated
(if I may call it) play—or reaction!—which is the mark,
or one of the marks, of your genius. Don't make too
much of rigours and indifferences, of consistencies and
vows; I have no greater affinity with associations and
academies than you—*a priori*; and yet I find myself glad
to have done the simple, civil, social *easiest* thing in

accepting my election—touched by the amenity and geniality of the thought that we shall probably *make something* collectively—in addition to what we may make individually. Don't think I want to harass or overbear you if I say that if these words still leave you cold I frankly don't want to let the matter go without seeing you over it. I would come up to Church Row—at any hour I might find you—after 3.30 p.m.—for the purpose, or would earnestly await you here at your own hour equally—with all the lively assurances of yours very faithfully

HENRY JAMES

55

WELLS TO JAMES

17, *Church Row, Hampstead.*
[*March* 25, 1912]

MY DEAR JAMES.

Your letter is most difficult to answer because I am not going to do as you wish. It's most difficult because not only have I a very deep affection for you but I have that snobbishness towards you which is quite honourable. I do look up to, and admire, and feel proud of my con-nexion with your beautiful fine abundant mind—I like to be about with you and in the same boat with you. If it was only you——. But I have an insurmountable objection to Literary or Artistic Academies as such, to any hierarchies, any suggestion of controls or fixed standards in these things. I feel it so strongly that indeed I would rather be outside the Academic Committee with Hall Caine, than in it with you and Gosse and Gilbert Murray and Shaw. This world of ours, I mean the world of creative and representative work we do, is I am convinced best anarchic.[1] Better the wild rush of Boomster and the Quack than the cold politeness of the established thing. And if I don't join you at any rate you take something of my heart into the Academic Committee. So far as that body does have a use and exert a good influence it will do it the better without my turbulent indiscretion. And if it was only a Friendship and not Academic and quasi-official and with a Royal Charter, how gladly would I come!

Forgive this ——— the only word to express my feelings is—disobedience, and believe me

Always yours,

H. G. WELLS.

[1] In later years Wells changed his mind and did join an organization of writers, the P.E.N., of which he became International President after the death of John Galsworthy. In that capacity, however, he continued to champion the "anarchic" world of literature, leading the P.E.N. clubs in their fight against Nazi and Communist attempts to regiment writers for political purposes.

56

JAMES TO WELLS

105 *Pall Mall, S.W.*
March 25th, 1912

MY DEAR WELLS.

Your letter is none the less interesting for being what,
alas, I believed it might be; in spite of which interest—or
in spite of which belief at least—here I am at you again!
I know perfectly what you mean by your indifference to
Academies and Associations, Bodies and Boards, on all
this ground of ours; no one should know better, as it is
precisely my own state of mind—really caring as I do for
nothing in the world but lonely patient virtue, which
doesn't seek that company. Nevertheless I fondly hoped
that it might end for you as it did, under earnest invitation, for me—in your having said and felt all those things
and then joined—for the general amenity and civility and
unimportance of the thing, giving it the benefit of the
doubt—for the sake of the good-nature. You will say
that you *had* no doubt and couldn't therefore act on any;
but that germ, alas, was what my letter sought to im-
plant—in addition to its not being a question of your
acting, but simply of your *not* (that is of your not refusing,
but simply lifting your oar and letting yourself float on
the current of acclamation.) There would be no question

L

of your being entangled or hampered, or even, I think, of your being bored; the common ground between all lovers and practitioners of our general form would be under your feet so *naturally* and not at all out of your way; and it wouldn't be you in the least who would have to take a step backward or aside, it would be *we* gravitating toward you, melting into your orbit as a mere more *direct* effect of the energy of your genius. Your plea of your being anarchic and seeing your work as such isn't in the least, believe me, a reason against; for (also believe me) you are essentially wrong about that! No talent, no imagination, no application of art, as great as yours are, is able not to make much less for anarchy than for a continuity and coherency much bigger than any disintegration. There's no representation, no picture (which is your form,) that isn't by its very nature preservation, association, and of a positive associational *appeal*—that is the very grammar of it; none that isn't thereby some sort of interesting or curious *order*: I utterly defy it in short not to make, all the anarchy in the world aiding, far more than it unmakes—just as I utterly defy the anarchic to express itself representationally, art aiding, talent aiding, the play of invention aiding, in short *you* aiding, without the grossest, the absurdest inconsistency. So it is that you are *in* our circle anyhow you can fix it, and with us always drawing more around (though always at a respectful and considerate distance,) fascinatedly to admire and watch— all to the greater glory of the English name, and the brave, as brave as possible English array; the latter brave even with the one American blotch upon it. Oh *patriotism!*—that mine, the mere paying guest in the house, should have its credit more at heart than its unnatural, its proud and perverse son! However, all this isn't to worry or to weary (I wish it *could!*) your ruthlessness; it's only to drop a sigh on my shattered dream that you might have come among us with as much freedom as grace. I prolong the sigh as I think how much you might have done for *our* freedom—and how little we could do against yours!

Don't answer or acknowledge this unless it may have miraculously moved you by some quarter of an inch. But then oh *do!*—though I must warn you that I shall in that case follow it up to the death! [1]

Yours all faithfully

HENRY JAMES.

[1] On the day following the writing of this letter, Henry James wrote to Edmund Gosse from the Reform Club: "My dear Gosse: This is just a word, on receipt of your note, to conclude the H. G. W. episode—of which absolutely nothing more will come. I wrote him last evening again, in an appealing and remonstrant way—it *interested* me to do so, and I thought there was perhaps a chance, or the fraction of one, of his response to two or three things I could still, with some point I felt, say to him. But his only response was to come into this place (Reform Club) today at luncheon time (I think he came on purpose to find me,) and let me see that he is absolutely immovable. I had a good deal of talk with him—though not, his refusal once perfectly *net*, about that, and without his having answered or met in any way any one of the things my second letter (any more for that matter than any of those my first) had put to him; and my sense that he is right about himself and that he wouldn't at all do among us from the moment

57

WELLS TO JAMES

17, *Church Row, Hampstead*
[*March 26, 1912*]

MY DEAR JAMES.

The other day at the *Reform* I saw you had backed a Candidate for admission and forthwith there was my dried pea for him. This afternoon my friend Emile Mond reminds me he is up for next Thursday, and unless Race, or the Man himself, stands in your way, may I ask for your dried pea in return.

Yours ever

H. G. WELLS

---

our whole literary side—or indeed any literary side anywhere—is a matter of such indifference to him as I felt it to be today—to an extent I hadn't been aware of. He has cut loose from literature clearly—practically altogether; he will still do a lot of writing probably—but it won't be *that*. This settles the matter, and I now agree with you settles it fortunately. He *had* decently to decline, and I think it decent of him to have felt that. My impression of him today cleared up many things. But I will tell you more about it. I won't pretend to speak of other things—to you who are at the centre of the cyclone. How interesting you will be—and how interesting everything else will be (God help all interests!) when you are next seen of Yours always Henry James."

58

JAMES TO WELLS

Lamb House, Rye, Sussex.

Dictated.

October 18th, 1912.

MY DEAR WELLS.

I have been sadly silent since having to wire you (nearly three weeks ago) my poor plea of inability to embrace your so graceful offer of an occasion for my at last meeting, in accordance with my liveliest desire, the eminent Arnold Bennett[1]; sadly in fact is a mild word for it, for I have cursed and raged, I have almost irrecoverably suffered—with all of which the end is not yet. I had just been taken, when I answered your charming appeal, with a violent and vicious attack of "Shingles"—under which I have lain prostrate till this hour. I don't shake it off—and perhaps you know how fell a thing it may be. I am precariously "up" and can do a little to beguile the black inconvenience of loss of time at a most awkward season by dealing after this graceless fashion with such arrears of smashed correspondence as I may so presume to patch up; but I mayn't yet plan for the repair of other

---

[1] James met Arnold Bennett little more than two months later in the office of his agent, J. B. Pinker. An account of the meeting is given in *The Journal of Arnold Bennett* under the date of 6 January 1913.

losses—I see no hope of my leaving home for many days, and haven't yet been further out of this house than to creep feebly about my garden, where a blest season has most fortunately reigned. A couple of months hence I go up to town to stay (I have taken a lease of a small unfurnished flat in Chelsea, on the river;) and there for the ensuing five or six months I shall aim at inducing you to bring the kind Bennett, whom I meanwhile cordially and ruefully greet, to partake with me of some modest hospitality.

Meanwhile if I've been deprived of you on one plane I've been living with you very hard on another; you may not have forgotten that you kindly sent me "Marriage" [1] (as you always so kindly render me that valued service;) which I've been able to give myself to at my less afflicted and ravaged hours. I have read you, as I always read you, and as I read no one else, with a complete abdication of all those "principles of criticism," canons of form, preconceptions of felicity, references to the idea of method or the sacred laws of composition, which I roam, which I totter, through the pages of others attended in some dim degree by the fond yet feeble theory of, but which I shake off, as I advance under your spell, with the most cynical inconsistency. For under your spell I do advance—save when I pull myself up stock still in order not to break it with so much as the breath of appreciation; I live with

[1] *Marriage*, published in 1912. For Wells's comments see pp. 217–20 below.

you and in you and (almost cannibal-like) *on* you, on you
H. G. W., to the sacrifice of your Marjories and your
Traffords, and whoever may be of their company; not
your treatment of them, at all, but, much more, their be-
fooling of you (pass me the merely scientific expression—
I mean your fine high action in view of the red herring of
lively interest they trail for you at their heels) becoming
thus of the essence of the spectacle for me, and nothing in
it all "happening" so much as these attestations of your
character and behaviour, these reactions of yours as you
more or less follow them, affect me as vividly happening.
I see you "behave" all along, much more than I see them
even when they behave, (as I'm not sure they behave *most*
in "Marriage") with whatever charged intensity or
accomplished effect; so that the ground of the drama is
somehow most of all in the adventure for *you*—not to
say *of* you—the moral, temperamental, personal, ex-
pressional, of your setting it forth; an adventure in fine
more appreciable to me than any of those you are by way
of letting *them* in for. I don't say that those you let them
in for don't interest me too, and don't "come off" and
people the scene and lead on the attention, about as much
as I can do with; but only, and always, that you beat them
on their own ground and that your "story", through the
five hundred pages, says more to me than theirs. You'll
find this perhaps a queer rigmarole of a statement, but I
ask of you to allow for it just now as the mumble, at best,
of an invalid; and wait a little till I can put more of my

hand on my sense. Mind you that the restriction I may seem to you to lay on my view of your work, still leaves that work more convulsed with life and more brimming with blood than any it is given me nowadays to meet. The point I have wanted to make is that I find myself absolutely unable, and still more unwilling, to approach you, or to take leave of you, in any projected light of criticism, in any judging or concluding, any comparing, in fact in any aesthetic or "literary", relation at all; and this in spite of the fact that the light of criticism is almost that in which I most fondly bask and that the amusement I consequently renounce is one of the dearest of all to me. I simply decline—that's the way the thing works— to pass you again through my cerebral oven for critical consumption: I consume you crude and whole and to the last morsel, cannibalistically, quite, as I say; licking the platter clean of the last possibility of a savour and remaining thus yours abjectly

HENRY JAMES.

59
WELLS TO JAMES

17, Church Row, Hampstead
[*October* 19, 1912]

MY DEAR JAMES,

I am glad to think you are a little better and distressed to think there should be a *bad* from which the better has to come. And it is beyond measure good of you to give attention to my book and to mingle as you do so much heartening kindliness with the wisest, most penetrating and guiding of criticism and reproof. I am, like so many poor ladies, destined to be worse before I am better; the next book is 'scandalously' bad in form, mixed pickles and I know it. It is I hope a prolonged acute disease rather than a chronic decay, and thereafter I will seek earnestly to make my pen lead a decent life, pull myself together, think of Form.

I hope very earnestly for your recovery. The *Reform Club* is a poor place without you.

Yours ever

H. G. WELLS

60

WELLS TO JAMES

Little Easton Rectory, Dunmow.

[*April* 9, 1913]

MY DEAR JAMES.

I've been reading of that Small Boy [1] with a dazzled admiration. As I grow up to a kind of technical understanding I begin to understand just what your amazing skill in atmospheres amounts to. I put the book beside your *American Scene*. You've given me a kind of life over there for myself, so that I half fancy that once round a street corner I saw Emerson. The other day I bought a kitchen clock of American origin, it had a little glass pane in its belly showing a colour smeared picture of Broadway—I should think about 1830 or 1840. I nearly broke into reminiscences at the sight.

How are you? I have been much abroad since Christmas but I hear you have been ill and are better and that you are installed in Chelsea. Bennett by this time is a member of the *Reform Club* and you have no doubt met him.

My warmest regards

H. G. WELLS

[1] The first volume of Henry James's autobiography, *A Small Boy and Others*, had just been published.

61

JAMES TO WELLS

21, Carlyle Mansions,
Cheyne Walk, S.W.
April 11th, 1913.

MY DEAR WELLS.

Your handsome tribute to the so presumptuous, so
fatuous Small Boy, whose cheeky argument is that he is
interesting—and on that *scale*—from the age of six
months to the age of 15–16 years exclusively (for the
present occasion) helps to relieve me from the fear of my
being *pilloried* for cheekiness—two or three other friends
having also reassured me not less kindly. Of course (or
I am afraid that) for myself the effort conforms to any
and every dealing with the thing I may have in mind—
that is with the necessity that that thing proceed for me
by the interest of the expression of it that *makes* it (*us*
interesting;) so that the matter becomes intensely a
literary and methodic one. In other words if literature as
life (or life as literature!) is great, Method is his prophet
—and the more so the more he (the prophet) works behind the veil—inscrutably, as it were, and with the "fun"
of secret harmonies.

I am *not*, meanwhile, very well, thank you!—with
fairly chronic pectoral (anginal—though not strictly

cardiac) distress, and have to live too carefully for any joy of freedom that the like of you (if there *be* any like of you!) knows and practises. But I go sometimes to the Reform—though almost only for victualling and in the evening—the relief of dining a little on other food than my cook's; for I never dine elsewhere. I am afraid that's a bad hour for finding Arnold B. but I shall try and track him there. I should like so to see him again. You clearly, are very valid and I the more impatiently await you—I mean out in the open. Yours all faithfully

HENRY JAMES

62

JAMES TO WELLS

Lamb House, Rye, Sussex.
September 21st, 1913.

MY DEAR WELLS.

I won't take time to tell you how touched I freshly am by the constancy with which you send me these wonderful books of yours—I am too impatient to let you know *how* wonderful I find this last.[1] I bare my head before the immense ability of it—before the high intensity with which your talent keeps itself interesting and which has made me absorb the so full-bodied thing in

[1] *The Passionate Friends*, published in September 1913.

deep and prolonged gustatory draughts. I am of my nature and by the effect of my own "preoccupations" a critical, a non-*naïf*, a questioning, worrying reader— and more than ever so at this end of time, when I jib altogether and utterly at the "fiction of the day" and find no company but yours and that, in a degree, of one or two others possible. To read a novel at all I perform afresh, to my sense, the act of writing it, that is of re-handling the subject accordingly to my own lights and over-scoring the author's form and pressure with my own vision and understanding of *the* way—this, of course I mean, when I *see* a subject in what he has done and feel its appeal to me as one: which I fear I very often don't. This produces reflections and reserves—it's the very measure of my attention and my interest; but there's nobody who makes these particular reactions less *matter* for me than you do, as they occur—who makes the whole apple-cart so run away that I don't care if I *don't* upset it and only want to stand out of its path and see it go. This is because you have so positive a process and method of your own (rare and *almost* sole performer to this tune roundabout us—in fact absolutely sole by the *force* of your exhibition) that there's an anxious joy in seeing what it does for you and with you. I find you perverse and I find you, on a whole side, unconscious, as I can only call it, but my point is that *with* this heart-breaking leak even sometimes so nearly playing the devil with the boat your talent remains so savoury and what you do so

substantial. I adore a rounded objectivity, a completely
and patiently achieved one, and what I mean by your
perversity and your leak is that your attachment to the
autobiographic form for the *kind of thing* undertaken, the
whole expression of actuality, "up to date," affects me as
sacrificing what I hold most dear, a precious effect of
perspective, indispensable, by my fond measure, to
beauty and authenticity. Where there needn't so much
be question of that, as in your hero's rich and roaring
impressionism, his expression of his own experience,
intensity and avidity as a whole, you are magnificent,
there your ability prodigiously triumphs and I grovel
before you. This is the way to take your book, I think—
with Stratton's *own* picture (I mean of himself and *his*
immediate world felt and seen with such exasperated and
ah such simplified impatiences,) as its subject exclusively.
So taken it's admirably sustained, and the life and force
and wit and humour, the imagination and arrogance and
genius with which you keep it up, are tremendous and
all your own. I think this projection of Stratton's rage
of reflection and observation and world-vision is in
its vividness and humour and general bigness of attack,
a most masterly thing to have done. His South Africa
etc. I think really sublime, and I can do beautifully with
his India and his China and America—I can do beautifully
with *him* and his "ideas" altogether—he is, and they are,
an immense success. Where I find myself doubting is
where I gather that you yourself see your subject more

particularly—and where I rather feel it escape me. That is, to put it simply—for I didn't mean to draw this out so much, and it's 2 o'clock a.m.!—the hero's prodigiously clever, foreshortened, impressionising *report* of the heroine and the relation (which last is, I take it, for you, the subject,) doesn't affect me as the real vessel of truth about them; in short, with all the beauty you have put into it—and much of it, especially at the last, is admirably beautiful—I don't care a fig for the hero's report *as an account of the matter*. You didn't mean a sentimental "love story" I take it—you meant ever so much more— and your way strikes me as *not* the way to give the truth about the woman of our hour. I don't think you *get* her, or at any rate give her, and all through one hears your remarkable—your wonderful!—reporting manner and voice (up to last week, up to last night,) and not, by my persuasion, hers. In those letters she writes at the last it's for me all Stratton, all masculinity and intellectual superiority (of the most real,) all a more dazzling journalistic talent than I observe any woman anywhere (with all respect to the cleverness they exhibit) putting on record. It isn't in these terms of immediate—that is of her pretended *own* immediate irony and own compre- hensive consciousness, that I see the woman made real at all; and by so much it is that I should be moved to take, as I say, such liberties of reconstruction. But I don't in the least *want* to take them, as I still more emphatically say—for what you *have* done has held me deliciously

intent and made me feel anew with thanks to the great
Author of all things what an invaluable form and in-
estimable art it is! Go on, go on and do it as you like, so
long as you *keep* doing it; your faculty is of the highest
price, your temper and your hand form one of the
choicest treasures of the time; my offensive remarks are
but the sign of my helpless subjugation and impotent
envy, and I am yours, my dear Wells, all gratefully and
faithfully

HENRY JAMES.

P.S. I find I don't know where to *address* you—
having heard you have left Hampstead, and not having noticed your country terms. So I am absurdly
reduced to the Mac[millan]s.

63

WELLS TO JAMES
*Little Easton Rectory, Dunmow
and 52 St. James's Court*
[*Sept.* 22, 1913]

MY DEAR JAMES,

You are the soul of generosity to me. That book is
gawky. It's legs and arms and misfitting clothes. It has
spots like an ill grown young man. Its manners are sly
and clumsy. It has been thrust into the world too soon.
I shall now be an artist. (The image alters here.) My
art is abortion—on the shelves of my study stand a little

vain-gloriously—thirty-odd premature births. Many re-
tain their gill slits. The most finished have still hare lips,
cleft palates, open crania. These are my children! But it
is when you write to me out of your secure and masterly
finish, out of your golden globe of leisurely (yet not slow)
and infinitely *easy* accomplishment that the sense of my
unworthiness and rawness is most vivid. Then indeed I
want to embrace your feet and bedew your knees with
tears—of quite unfruitful penitence.

Yours ever,

H. G. WELLS

64

JAMES TO MRS. WELLS

21 Carlyle Mansions,
Cheyne Walk, S.W.
March 21st, 1914.

DEAR MRS. WELLS.

Your invitation is delightfully engaging, but will you
allow an ancient sage, apt to find himself too fat and scant
o' breath for the general pace, just to leave the beautiful
question open for the moment and a little dependent on
his *then* (his Tuesday next) measure of his shrunken
powers? He would like extremely to present himself, and
has the most romantic recollection of those brave bright
revels of a couple of years ago. In short he cherishes a
tremulous hope, and if he is beaten back please understand that it will have been only after an attitude of

M

remarkable, if obscure, gallantry. I quite inordinately want to see H.G., whom I sympathetically greet, and am yours and his all faithfully

HENRY JAMES

65

HENRY JAMES

"The Younger Generation" [1]

PART ONE

We feel it not to be the paradox it may at the first blush seem that the state of the novel in England at the present time is virtually very much the state of criticism itself; and this moreover, at the risk perhaps of some added appearance of perverse remark, by the very reason that we see criticism so much in abeyance. So far as we miss it altogether, how and why does its "state" signify, and why and how can it or should it, as an absent force, enjoy a relation to that constant renewal of our supply of fiction which is a present one so far as a force at all?

The relation is this, in the fewest words—that no equal outpouring of matter into the mould of literature, or what roughly passes for such, has been noted to live its life and maintain its flood, its level at least of quantity and mass,

[1] *The Times Literary Supplement* 19 March and 2 April 1914, pp. 133–134 and 137–158.

in such free and easy independence of critical attention. It constitutes a condition and a perversity on the part of this element to remain so irresponsive before an appeal so vociferous at least and so incessant; therefore how can such a neglect of occasion, so careless a habit in spite of marked openings, be better described than as responsibility declined in the face of disorder? The rush of "production" has at any rate so exceeded the activity of control that this latter anxious agent, first alarmed but then indifferent, has been forced backward out of the gate, leaving the contents of the reservoir to boil and evaporate. Never was the reservoir so bubblingly and noisily full, at any rate by the superficial measure of life; and this tide, swollen by extravagant cheap contribution, the increase of affluents turbid and unstrained, shows us the number of ways in which the democratic example, once gathering momentum, sets its mark on societies and seasons that stand in its course. Nowhere is that example written larger than in the New Novel.

I

The new, or at least the young, novel is up and doing with the best faith, clearly, and the highest spirits in the world; if we but extend a little our measure of youth indeed, as we are happily more and more disposed to, we may speak of it as already chin-deep in trophies. The men who are not so young as the youngest were but the other day very little older than these. Mr. Joseph Conrad, Mr.

Maurice Hewlett and Mr. Galsworthy, Mr. H. G. Wells
and Mr. Arnold Bennett have not quite perhaps the early
bloom of Mr. Hugh Walpole, Mr. Gilbert Cannan, Mr.
Compton Mackenzie and Mr. D. H. Lawrence; but the
spring unrelaxed is still, to our perception, in their step,
and we see two or three of them sufficiently related to the
still newer generation in a quasi-parental way to make our
whole enumeration as illustrational as we wish it. The
author of "Tono-Bungay" and of "The New Machiavelli," and the author of "The Old Wives' Tale" and of
"Clayhanger," have practically launched the boat in
which we admire the fresh play of oar of the author of
"The Duchess of Wrexe" and the documented aspect exhibited successively by "Round the Corner," by
"Carnival" and "Sinister Street," and even by "Sons and
Lovers," however much we may find Mr. Lawrence, we
confess, hang in the dusty rear. We bracket together Mr.
Wells and Mr. Bennett for the particular reason that with
the sharpest differences of character and range they yet
come together under our so convenient measure of value
by saturation. Each is ideally immersed in his own body
of reference, in a closer notation, a sharper specification
of the signs of life and consciousness in the human scene
and the human subject than the three or four generations
before them had at all been moved to insist on. They had
insisted, these generations, on almost nothing whatever;
what was to come to them had come, an enormous afflu-
ence and freshness at its best, and to our continued appre-

ciation as well as to the honour of their sweet susceptibility, because again and again the great miracle of genius
took place, while they gaped, in their social and sentimental sky. For our own time that miracle has not been
markedly renewed, but we have learned a little to insist,
and we thus get back on one hand something of what we
have lost on the other. To this nearer view of commoner
things the authors we have named, taking one with
another, strike us as having gathered themselves up in a
spirit never yet apparent on our literary scene, and with
an instinctive divination, we make out, of what had most
kept their predecessors clear of it.

What had this lion in the path been, we see them after
a fashion ask themselves, but the fond superstition that
the key of the situation, of each and every one that could
turn up for the novelist, was the sentimental key, which
might fit into no single lock of the great chamber of close-
ness and freshness at all? Was it not for all the world as if
even the brightest practitioners of the past, those we now
distinguish as saved for glory in spite of themselves, had
been as sentimental as they could, or, to give the trick
another name, as romantic and thereby as shamelessly
"dodgy"?—just in order not to *be* close and fresh, not to
be authentic, as that takes time and trouble, takes talent,
and you can be sentimental, you can be romantic, you
can be dodgy, alas! not a bit less on the footing of
genius than on the footing of mediocrity or even of
imbecility? The sentimental habit and the spirit of

romance stood out to sea as far as possible, through all the Victorian age, the moment the shore appeared to offer the least difficulty to hugging; and that age bristled with examples of this showy retreat caught in the very act. All revolutions have been prepared in spite of their so often striking us as sudden; and so it was doubtless that, when scarce longer ago than the other day, Mr. Arnold Bennett had the fortune to lay his hand on a general scene and a cluster of agents deficient to a peculiar degree in properties that might interfere with the desirable density of illustration—deficient, that is, in such connexions as might carry the imagination off to some sport on its own account—we recognized at once a set of conditions auspicious to the newer kind of appeal. The state of inordinate possession on the chronicler's part, the mere state as such and as an energy directly exhibited, became the whole interest, neither more nor less, became the sense and the meaning and the picture and the drama, and seemed at first all so sufficiently to constitute them that it scarce mattered what they were in themselves. What we recognize the author as doing is simply recording his possession or, to repeat our more emphatic term, his saturation; and to see him as virtually shut up to that process is a note of all the more moment that we see our selected cluster of interesting juniors, and whether by his direct action on their collective impulse or not, embroiled, as we venture to call it, in the same predicament. They squeeze out to the utmost the plump and more or less juicy orange of a particular acquainted state and let this affirmation of energy, however directed or undirected, constitute for them the "treatment" of the theme.

II

Nothing is further from us, of course, than to undervalue the particular acquainted state, that of saturation and possession, however it may have been brought about; for it represents on behalf of the novelist, as on that of any painter of things seen, felt or imagined, just one-half of his authority, the other half being represented, naturally, by the application he is inspired to make of that advantage. Therefore this fine secured half is so much gained at the start; and the fact of its brightly being there may really by itself project upon the course colour and form enough to make us at times, under the genial force, almost not miss the answer to the question of application. When the author of "Clayhanger" has put down upon the table, in dense unconfused array, every fact required to make the life of the Five Towns press upon us and to make our sense of it, so full fed, content us, we may very well go on for the time in the captive condition, the beguiled and bemused condition, the acknowledgment of which is in general our highest tribute to the temporary master of our sensibility. Nothing at such moments—or rather at the end of them, when the end begins to threaten—may be of a more curious strain than

the dawning unrest that suggests to us fairly our first
critical comment: "Yes, yes; but is this *all*? These are
the circumstances of the interest—we see, we see; but
where is the interest itself, where and what is its centre and
how are we to measure it in relation to *that*?"

There are people to tell us in plenty of course that to
"measure" an interest is none of our affair; that we have
but to take it on the cheapest and easiest terms and be
thankful; and that if by our very confession we have been
led the imaginative dance the music has done for us all
that it pretends to. Which words, however, have only to
happen to be for us the most unintelligent conceivable
not in the least to arrest our wonderment as to where our
bedrenched consciousness may still not awkwardly leave
us for the pleasure of appreciation. The more appreciation plays up in us, the more we recognise and are able to
number the sources of our enjoyment, the greater is the
provision for security in that attitude, which corresponds,
by the same stroke, with the reduced danger of waste in
the undertaking to amuse us. It all comes back to our
amusement, and to the noblest surely, on the whole, that
we know; and it is in the very nature of clinging appreciation not to sacrifice consentingly a single shade of the
art that makes for this blessing. From our solicitudes
spring our questions, and not least the one to which we
give ourselves for the moment here—this moment of our
being regaled as never yet with the fruits of the movement
(if the name be not of too pompous an application where

the flush and the heat of accident too seem so candidly to look forth), in favour of the "expression of life" in terms as loose as may pretend to an effect of expression at all. The relegation of terms to the limbo of delusions outlived so far as ever really cultivated becomes of necessity, it will be plain, the great mark of the faith that for the novelist to show he "knows all about" a certain congeries of aspects, the more numerous within their mixed circle the better, is thereby to set in motion with due intensity the pretension to interest. The state of knowing all about whatever it may be has thus only to become consistently and abundantly active to pass for his supreme function; and to its so becoming active few difficulties appear to be described, so great may on occasion become the mere excitement and exhilaration of activity.

III

We should have only to remount the current with a certain energy to come straight up against Tolstoy as the great illustrative master-hand on all this ground of disconnexion of method from matter—and so prompt in us the remark that of all great painters of the social picture it was given that epic genius most to serve admirably as a rash adventurer and a "caution," and execrably, pestilentially, as a model. In this strange union of relations he stands alone: from no other great projector of the human image and the human idea is so much truth to be extracted under an equal leakage of its value, that is an equal failure to exhibit, to present the value. All the proportions in him are so much the largest that the drop of attention to our cases nearer at hand might by its violence leave little of the principle alive; which fact need not disguise from us none the less that as we take Mr. H. G. Wells and Mr. Arnold Bennett to derive, by multiplied if diluted transmissions, from the great Russian, so, observing the distances, we may profitably detect an unexhausted influence in our minor, our still considerably less rounded vessels. Highly attaching the game, as might be, of inquiring as to the centre of the interest or the sense of the whole in "The Passionate Friends" or in "The Old Wives' Tale," after having sought those luxuries in vain through the general length and breadth of "War and Peace"; this as preparing us to address a like friendly challenge to Mr. Cannan's "Round the Corner," say, or to Mr. Lawrence's "Sons and Lovers" —should we wish to be very friendly to Mr. Lawrence— or to Mr. Hugh Walpole's "Duchess of Wrexe," or even to Mr. Compton Mackenzie's "Sinister Street" and "Carnival"; discernibly, we hasten to add, though certain betrayals of a controlling idea and a pointed intention do comparatively gleam out of the two fictions last named. "The Old Wives' Tale" is the history of two sisters, daughters of a prosperous draper in a Staffordshire town, who, separating early in life, through the flight of one of them to Paris with an ill-chosen husband and the confirmed and prolonged local pitch of the career of the other, are reunited, conclusively, by the return of the fugitive after much Parisian experience and by her gradually pacified acceptance of the conditions of her birthplace. The divided current flows together again, and the chronicle closes with the simple drying up determined by the death of the sisters. That is all; the canvas is covered, ever so closely and vividly covered, by the exhibition of innumerable small facts and aspects, at which we assist with the most comfortable sense of their substantial truth. The sisters, and more particularly the less adventurous, are at home in their author's mind; they sit and move at their ease in the square chamber of his attention to a degree beyond which the production of that ideal harmony between creature and creator could scarcely go, and all by an art of demonstration so familiar and so "quiet" that the truth and the poetry, to use Goethe's distinction, melt utterly together, and we see no difference between the subject of the show and the showman's "feeling," let alone the showman's manner, about it.

This felt identity of the elements—because we at least consciously feel—becomes in the novel we refer to, and not less in "Clayhanger," which our words equally describe, a source for us of abject confidence, confidence truly *so* abject in the solidity of every appearance that it may be said to represent our whole relation to the work and completely to exhaust our reaction upon it. "Clayhanger"—of the two fictions even the more densely

packed with all the evidence in what we should call the
case presented did we but learn meanwhile for what case,
or for a case of what, to take it—inscribes the annals, the
private more particularly, of a provincial printer in a considerable way of business, beginning with his early boyhood and going on to the complications of his maturity.
This most monumental of Mr. Bennett's recitals, taking
it with the supplement of "Hilda Lessways," already before us, and with more of the catalogue to follow, is so
describable through its being a monument exactly not to
an idea, a pursued and captured meaning, or, in short, to
anything whatever but just simply of the quarried and
gathered material it happens to contain, the stones and
bricks and rubble and cement and promiscuous con-
stituents of every sort that have been heaped in it and
thanks to which it quite massively piles itself up. Our
perusal and our enjoyment are our watching of the growth
of the pile and of the capacity, industry, energy, with
which the operation is directed. While we watch and
wait we are amused—were it not for that, truly, we should
wonder still more; but we may ask ourselves, as has
already been noted, why on such ambiguous terms we
should consent to be, and why the practice doesn't at a
given moment break down. Our answer then brings us
back to that many-fingered grasp of the orange that the
author squeezes. This particular orange is of the largest
and most rotund, and his trust in the consequent flow
of its nature communicative. Such is the case always, and

most naturally, with that air of a person who has something, who at the very least has much, to tell us: we *like* to
be affected by it, we meet it half-way and lend ourselves,
sinking in it up to the chin. Up to the chin only, indeed,
beyond doubt; we even then feel our head emerge, for
judgment and articulate question; and it is from that
position that we remind ourselves how the real reward of
our patience is still to come—the reward attending not
at all the immediate sense of immersion, but reserved for
the after-sense, which is a very different matter, whether
in the form of a glow or of a chill.

IV

If Mr. Bennett's tight rotundity, then, is of the hand-
somest size and his manipulation of it so firm, what are
we to say of Mr. Wells's, who, a novelist very much as
Lord Bacon was a philosopher, affects us as taking all
knowledge for his province and as inspiring in us to the
very highest degree the confidence enjoyed by himself?—
enjoyed, we feel, with a breadth with which it has been
given no one of his fellow-craftsmen to enjoy anything.
If confidence alone could lead utterly captive we should
all be huddled in a bunch at Mr. Wells's heels, which is
indeed where we *are* abjectly gathered, so far as that force
does operate. It is literally Mr. Wells's own mind, and
the experience of his own mind, incessant and extraordinarily various, extraordinarily reflective, even with
all sorts of conditions made, of whatever he may expose

it to, that forms the reservoir tapped by him, that suffices for his exhibition of grounds of interest. The more he knows and knows, or at any rate learns and learns—the more, in other words, he establishes his saturation—the greater is our impression of his holding it good enough for us, such as we are, that he shall but turn out his mind and its contents upon us by any free familiar gesture and as from a high window forever open (Mr. Wells having as many windows as an agent who has bought up the lot of the most eligible to retail for a great procession).

Such things as "The New Machiavelli," "Marriage," "The Passionate Friends," are so very much more attestations of the presence of material than of an interest in the use of it that we ask ourselves again and again why so fondly neglected a state of leakage comes not to be fatal to *any* provision of quantity, or even to stores more specially selected for the ordeal than Mr. Wells's always strike us as being. Is not the witnessed pang of waste, in fact, great just in proportion as we are touched by our author's fine offhandedness as to the value of the stores, about which he can for the time make us believe what he will? So that, to take an example susceptible of brief statement, we wince at a certain quite peculiarly gratuitous sacrifice to the casual in "Marriage" very much as at seeing some fine and indispensable little part of a mechanism slip through profane fingers and lose itself. Who does not remember what ensues after a little upon the aviational descent of the hero of that fiction into the garden occupied, in company with her parents, by the young lady with whom he is to fall in love?—and this even though the whole opening scene so constituted, with all the comedy hares its function appears to be to start, remains with its back squarely turned, æsthetically speaking, to the quarter in which the picture develops. The point for our mortification is that by one of the first steps in this development, the first impression on him having been made, the hero accidentally meets the heroine, of a summer eventide, in a leafy lane which supplies them with the happiest occasion to pursue their acquaintance—or in other words supplies the author with the liveliest consciousness (as we feel it should be) that just so the relation between the pair, its seed already sown, and the fact of that bringing about all that is still to come, pushes aside whatever veil and steps forth into life. To show it step forth and affirm itself as a relation, what is this but the interesting function of the whole passage, on the performance of which what follows is to hang? —and yet who can say that when the ostensible sequence *is* presented, and our young lady, encountered again by her stirred swain, under cover of night, in a favouring wood, is at once encompassed by his arms and pressed to his lips and heart (for celebration thus of their third meeting), we do not assist at a well-nigh heartbreaking miscarriage of "effect"? We see effect, invoked in vain, simply stand off unconcerned; effect not having been at all consulted in advance, she is not to be secured on such

terms. And her presence would so have redounded—
perfectly punctual creature that she is on a made appoint-
ment and a clear understanding—to the advantage of all
concerned. The bearing of the young man's act is all in
our having begun to conceive it as possible, begun even
to desire it, in the light of what has preceded; therefore
if the participants have *not* been shown us as on the way
to it, nor the question of it made beautifully to tremble
for us in the air, its happiest connexions fail and we but
stare at it mystified. The instance is undoubtedly
trifling, but in the infinite complex of such things resides
for a work of art the shy virtue, shy at least till wooed
forth, of the whole susceptibility.

The case of Mr. Wells might take us much further—
such remarks as there would be to make, say, in such a
connexion as a due understanding, on the part of "The
Passionate Friends" (not as associated persons but as a
composed picture), of what that composition is specific-
ally about and where, for treatment of this interest, it
undertakes to find its centre; all of which, we are willing,
however, to grant, falls away before the large assurance
and incorrigible levity with which this adventurer carries
his lapses, for more of an adventurer as he is than any
other of the company. The composition, as we have
called it, heaven save the mark! is simply at any and
every moment "about" Mr. Wells's own most general adventure; which is quite enough while it preserves, as we
trust it will long continue to do, its present robust pitch.

V

We have already noted that "Round the Corner," Mr. Gilbert Cannan's liveliest appeal to our attention, belongs to the order of *constatations* pure and simple; to the degree that as a document of that nature and of that rigour the book could perhaps not more completely affirm itself. When we have said that it puts on record the "tone," the manners, the general domestic proceedings and *train de vie* of an amiable clergyman's family established in one of the more sordid quarters of a big black northern city, of the Liverpool or Manchester complexion, we have advanced as far in the way of descriptive statement as the interesting work seems to warrant. For it *is* interesting, in spite of its leaving itself on our hands with so consistent an indifference to any question of a charmed application springing from it all as places it in the forefront of its type. Again as under the effect of Mr. Bennett's major productions our sole inference is that things, the things disclosed, *go on and on, in any given case, in spite of everything*—this serving as a sort of formula of the show; with Mr. Cannan's one discernible care perhaps being for her extraordinarily much, in the particular example here before him, they were able to go on in spite of. The conception, the presentation of this enormous inauspicious amount as bearing upon the collective career of the Folyats is, we think, as near as the author comes at any point to betraying an awareness of a

N

subject. Yet again, though so little encouraged or "backed" a subject after a fashion makes itself, even as it has made itself in "The Old Wives' Tale," in "Clay-hanger," and in "Sons and Lovers," where, as we have hinted, any assistance rendered us for a view of one most comfortably enjoys its absence; and in Mr. Hugh Walpole's newest novel, where we wander scarcely less with our hand in no guiding grasp, but where the author's good disposition to provide us with what we lack if he only knew how constitutes in itself such a pleading liberality. We seem to see him in this spirit lay again and again a flowered carpet for our steps. If we do not include Mr. Compton Mackenzie to the same extent in our generalisation it is really because we note a difference in him, a difference in favour of his care for the application. We catch preoccupations at work in "Sinister Street," and withal in "Carnival," the brush of which we in other quarters scarce even suspect and at some of which it will presently be of profit to glance. "I answer for it, you know," we seem at any rate to hear Mr. Gilbert Cannan say with an admirably genuine young pessimism, "I answer for it that they were really like that, odd or un-pleasant or uncontributive, and therefore tiresome, as it may strike you"; and the charm of Mr. Cannan, so far as up and down the rank we disengage a charm, is that we take him at his word. His guarantee, his straight com-munication, of his general truth is a value; and values are rare—the flood of fiction is apparently capable of running hundreds of miles without a single glint of one—and thus in default of satisfaction we get stopgaps and are thankful often under a genial touch to get even so much.

The value indeed is crude, it would be quadrupled were it only wrought and shaped; yet it has still the rude dignity that it counts to us for experience, or at least for what we call under our present pitch of sensibility force of impression. The experience, we feel, is ever something to conclude upon, while the impression is content to wait; to wait, say, in the spirit in which we must accept this younger bustle if we accept it at all, the spirit of it serving as a rather presumptuous lesson to us in patience. While we wait, again, we are amused—not in the least, also to repeat, up to the notch of our conception of amusement, which draws upon still other forms and sources, but none the less for the wonder, the intensity, the actuality, the probity of the vision. This is much as in "Clayhanger" and in "Hilda Lessways," where, independently of the effect, so considerably rendered, of the long lapse of time, always in this type of recital a source of amusement in itself, and certainly of the noblest, we get such an admirably substantial thing as the collective image of the Orgreaves, the local family in whose ample lap the amenities and the humanities so easily sit, for Mr. Bennett's evocation and his protagonist's recognition, and the manner of the presentation of whom, with the function and relation of the picture at large, strikes such a note of felicity, achieves such a simulation of sense, as the author

should never again be excused for treating, that is, for
neglecting, as beyond his range. Here figures signally the
interesting case of a compositional office absolutely discharged by mere multiplication, the flow of the facts; the
Orgreaves, in "Clayhanger," are there, by what we make
out, but for "life," for general life only, and yet, with their
responsibility under any general or inferential meaning
entirely unmarked, come doubtless as near squaring
æsthetically with the famous formula of the "slice of life"
as any example that could be adduced; happening moreover as they probably do to owe this distinction to their
coincidence at once with reality and with "charm";
a fact æsthetically rare and delightful. For we attribute
the bold stroke they represent much more to Mr. Arnold
Bennett's æsthetic instinct than to anything like a calcula-
tion of his bearings, and more to his state of thorough
acquaintance, as we may again put it, than to all other
causes together: which strikingly enough shows how
much complexity of interest may be simulated by mere
presentation of material, mere squeezing of the orange,
when the material happens to be "handsome" or the
orange to be sweet.

PART TWO

The orange of our persistent simile is in Mr. Hugh
Walpole's hands very remarkably sweet—a quality we
recognize in it even while reduced to observing that the
squeeze pure and simple, the fond, the lingering, the

reiterated squeeze, constitutes as yet his main perception of method. He enjoys in a high degree the consciousness of saturation, and is on such serene and happy terms with it as almost make of critical interference, in so bright an air, an assault on personal felicity.

Full of material is thus the author of "The Duchess of Wrexe," and of a material which we should describe as the consciousness of youth were we not rather disposed to call it a peculiar strain of the extreme unconsciousness. Mr. Walpole offers us indeed a rare and interesting case— we see about the field none other like it; the case of a positive identity between the spirit, not to say the time of life or stage of experience, of the aspiring artist, and the field itself of his vision. "The Duchess of Wrexe" reeks with youth and the love of youth and the con- fidence of youth—youth taking on with a charming exuberance the fondest costume or disguise, that of an adventurous and voracious felt interest, interest in life, in London, in society, in character, in Portland-place, in the Oxford-circus, in the afternoon tea-table, in the torrid weather, in fifty other immediate things as to which its passion and its curiosity are of the sincerest. The won- derful thing is that these latter forces operate, in their way, without yet being disengaged and hand-free—dis- engaged, that is, from their state of *being* young, with its billowy mufflings and other soft obstructions, the state of being present, being involved and aware, close "up against" the whole mass of possibilities, being in short

intoxicated with the mixed liquors of suggestion. In the
fumes of this acute situation Mr. Walpole's "subject
matter" is bathed; the situation being so far more his own
and that of a juvenility reacting, in the presence of everything, "for all it is worth," than the devised and con-
structed one, however he may circle about some such
cluster, that every cupful of his excited flow tastes three
times as much of his temperamental freshness as it does
of this, that or the other character or substance, above all
of this, that or the other bunch of antecedents and references, supposed to be reflected in it. All of which does
not mean, we hasten to add, that the author of "The
Duchess of Wrexe" has not the gift of life; but only that
he strikes us as having received it, straight from nature,
with such a concussion as to have kept the boon at the
stage of violence—so that, fairly pinned down by it, he is
still embarrassed for passing it on. On the day he shall
have worked free of this primitive predicament, the con-
vulsion itself, there need be no doubt of his exhibiting
matter into which method may learn how to bite. The
tract affects us meanwhile as more or less virgin snow, and
we look with interest and suspense for the foot-print of a
process.

If these remarks represent all the while, further, that
the performances we have glanced at, with others besides, lead our attention on, we hear ourselves the more
naturally asked what it is then that we expect or want, confessing as we do that we have been in a manner in-

terested, even though, from case to case, in a varying degree, and that Thackeray, Turgenieff, Balzac, Dickens, Anatole France, no matter who, cannot do more than interest. Let us therefore concede to the last point that small mercies are better than none, that there are latent within the critic numberless liabilities to being "squared" —the extent to which he may on occasion betray his price!—together with so great a preference for being pleased over not being, that you may again and again see him assist with avidity at the attempt of the slice of life to butter itself thick. But how can it be anything but illus- trational of the loaf, and how can illustration not imme- diately bristle with every sign of the expected and related state? It breaks down when reference, otherwise applica- tion, runs short, so that we look ever for the supreme reference that shall avert the bankruptcy of sense. The weakness of the spell of the happy-go-lucky is apparent at a glance. There faces us all the while the fact that the act of consideration as an incident of the æsthetic pleasure, consideration confidently knowing us to *have* sooner or later to arrive at it, may be again and again postponed, but can never hope not sometime to fall due.

I

It is doubtless fortunate that at the very moment of our urging this truth we should happen to be regaled with a really supreme specimen of the part playable, for our in- tenser interest, by a case of the exhibition of method at any price. Mr. Joseph Conrad's "Chance" places the author absolutely alone as the votary of the way to do a thing that shall make it undergo most doing. The way to do it that shall make it undergo least is the line on which we are mostly now used to see prizes carried off; so that the author of "Chance" gathers up on this showing all sorts of comparative distinction.

What the difficulties Mr. Conrad has "elected" to face consist of we should have to diverge a little to say, and should even then probably but lose ourselves in the dim question of why so special, eccentric and desperate a course, so deliberate a plunge into threatened frustration, should alone have seemed open. It has been the course, so far as three words may here serve, of his so multiplying his creators or, as we are now fond of saying, producers, as to make them almost more numerous and quite emphatically more material than the creatures and the production itself in whom and which we by the general law of fiction expect such agents to lose themselves. We take for granted by the general law of fiction a primary author, take him so much for granted that we forget him in proportion as he works upon us, and that he works upon us most in fact by making us forget him. Mr. Conrad's first care, adversely to this, is expressly to posit or set up a reciter, a definite responsible intervening first person singular, possessed of infinite sources of reference, who immediately proceeds to set up another to the end that this other may conform again to the practice, and that even at that point the bridge over to the creature, or in other words to the situation or the subject, the thing "produced," shall, if the fancy takes it, once more and yet once more glory in a gap. It is easy to see how heroic the undertaking of an effective fusion becomes on these terms, fusion between what we are to know and that prodigy of our knowing which is ever half the very beauty of the atmosphere of authenticity; from the moment the reporters are thus multiplied from pitch to pitch the tone of each, especially as "rendered" by his precursor in the series, becomes for the prime poet of all an immense question—these circumferential tones having not only to be such individually separate notes but to keep so clear of the others, the central, the numerous and various voices of the agents proper, those expressive of the action itself and in whom the objectivity resides. We usually escape the worst of this difficulty of a tone *about* the tone of our characters, our projected performers, by keeping it single, keeping it down and thereby comparatively impersonal and inscrutable; which is what a creative force, in its blest fatuity, likes to be. But the omniscience, remaining indeed nameless, though constantly active, which is set in motion from the first page and which then, on the same one, sets Marlow's omniscience in motion, insisting on a reciprocity with it throughout, this original omniscience invites consideration of itself only in a degree less than that in which Marlow's own invites it; and Marlow's own is a prolonged hovering flight of the subjective over the outstretched ground of the case exposed. We make out this ground, only through the shadow cast by the flight, clarify it though the real author visibly reminds himself again and again that he must—all the more that, as if by some tremendous forecast of future applied science, the upper aeroplane causes another, as we have said, to depend from it and that one still another; these dropping shadow after shadow, to the no small eclipse of intrinsic colour and form and whatever, upon the passive expanse.

What shall we most call Mr. Conrad's method accordingly but his attempt to clarify *quand même*—ridden as he has been, we perceive at the end of fifty pages of "Chance," by such a danger of steeping his matter in perfect eventual obscuration as we recall no other artist's consenting to with an equal grace. This grace, which presently comes over us as the sign of the whole business, is Mr. Conrad's gallantry itself, and the shortest account of the rest of the connexion for our present purpose is that his gallantry is thus his success. It literally strikes us that his volume sets in motion more than anything else a drama in which his own system and his combined eccentricities of recital represent the protagonist in face of powers leagued against it, and of which the *dénouement* gives us the system fighting in triumph, though with its back desperately to the wall, and laying the powers piled up at its feet. This frankly has been our spectacle, our

suspense and our thrill; with the one flaw on the round-
ness of it all the fact that the predicament was not imposed
rather than invoked, was not the effect of a challenge
from without, but that of a mystic impulse from within.
The indispensable fusion we spoke of above has taken
place, or at any rate *a* fusion, only it has been transferred
in wonderous fashion to an unexpected, and on the whole
more limited plane of operation; it has been effected not
on the ground but in the air, not between our writer's idea
and his machinery, but between the different parts of his
genius itself. His genius is what is left over from the
other, the compromised and compromising quantities,
and the residuum has the form not of such and such a
number of images discharged and ordered, but that rather
of a wandering, circling, yearning imaginative *faculty*,
encountered in its habit as it lives and diffusing itself as a
presence or a tide, a noble sociability of vision. So we
have as the force that fills the cup just the high-water mark
of a beautiful and generous mind in conditions comparatively thankless—thoroughly, unweariedly, yet at
the same time ever so elegantly at play, and doing more
for itself than it succeeds in getting done for it.

II

One of his compositional consequences there is, however, that has had most to do with making his pages
differ in texture, and to the very first glance, from that
struggle of ungoverned verbiage which leads us up and

down those of his fellow fabulists in general on a vain hunt for some projected mass of truth, some solidity of substance, as to which the deluge of "dialogue," the flooding report of words pretendedly spoken, shall have learned the art of being merely illustrational. What first springs from any form of real attention, no matter which, we on a comparison so made quickly perceive to be a practical challenge of the preposterous claim of this most fatuous of the luxuries of looseness to acquit itself with authority of the structural and compositional office. Infinitely valid and vivid as illustration, it altogether depends for dignity and sense upon our state of possession of its historic preliminaries, its promoting conditions, its supporting ground; that is upon our waiting occupancy of the chamber it proposes to light and which, when no other source of effect is more indicated, it doubtless quite inimitably fills with life. Then its relation to what encloses and confines and, in its sovereign interest, finely compresses it, offering it constituted aspects, surfaces, presences, faces and figures of the matter we are either generally or acutely concerned with to play over and hang upon, is the making of its importance—it has flowered from the soil prepared and sheds back its richness into the field of cultivation. It is interesting, in short, only when no other mode of presentation is equally or is more so; which other modes of presentation have a constant liability to be. We need, of course, scarce expressly note that the play, as distinguished from the novel, lives ex-

clusively on the spoken word—not on the report of the
thing said, but, directly and audibly, on that very thing;
that it thrives by its law on the exercise under which the
novel hopelessly collapses when the attempt is made dis-
proportionately to impose it. It is no less apparent that
the novel may be fundamentally *organized*—such things
as "The Egoist" and "The Awkward Age" are with us
to exemplify; but in this case it adheres unconfusedly to
that logic and has nothing to say to any other. Were it
not for a second exception then, still beyond "Chance,"
and one at this season quite pertinent, Mr. Conrad's tale
would be as happy an instance as we might just now put
our hand on of the automatic working of a scheme unfavourable to that treatment of the colloquy by endless
dangling strings which makes the current "story" in
general so figure to us a porcupine of extravagant yet
abnormally relaxed bristles.

III

The exception we speak of would be "The Custom of
the Country," in which, as in Mrs. Wharton's other
fictions, we recognize the happy fact of an abuse of no
one of the resources it enjoys at the expense of the others;
the whole series offering as general an example of dialogue
flowering and not weeding, illustrational and not itself
starved of illustration, or starved of referability and association, which is the same thing, as meets the eye in any
glance which leaves Mr. Wells at Mr. Wells's best-

inspired hour out of our account. The truth is, however, that Mrs. Wharton is herself here out of our account, even as we have easily recognised Mr. Galsworthy and Mr. Maurice Hewlett to be; these three authors, with whatever differences between them, remaining essentially votaries of selection and intention and being embodiments thereby, in each case, of some state over and above that simple state of possession of much evidence, that confused conception of what the "slice" of life must consist of, which forms the text of our remarks.

Mrs. Wharton, *her* conception of the "slice" so clarified and cultivated, would herself of course form a text in quite another connexion, as Mr. Hewlett and Mr. Galsworthy would do each in his own, which we abstain from specifying; but there are two or three grounds on which the author of "Ethan Frome," "The Valley of Decision" and "The House of Mirth," whom we brush by with reluctance, would point the moral of the treasure of amusement sitting in the lap of method with a felicity peculiarly her own. If one of these is that she, too, has clearly a saturation—which it would be ever so interesting to determine and appreciate—we have it from her not in the crude state but in the extract, the extract that makes all the difference for our sense of an artistic economy, the thing in the world surely on which our richest amusement most depends. If the extract, as would appear, is the result of an artistic economy, as the latter is its logical motive, so we find it associated in Mrs. Wharton with such appeals to our interest, for instance, as the fact that, absolutely sole among our students of this form, she suffers, she even encourages, her expression to flower into some sharp image or figure of her thought when that will make the thought more finely touch us. Her step, without straying, encounters the living analogy, which she gathers, in passing, without awkwardness of pause, and which the page then carries on its breast as a trophy plucked by a happy adventurous dash, a token of spirit and temper as well as a proof of vision. We note it as one of the *kinds* of proof of vision that most fail us in that comparative desert of the inselective where our imagination has itself to hunt out or call down (often among strange witnessed flounderings or sand-storms) such analogies as may mercifully, which is a little more vividly, "put" the thing.

Mrs. Wharton not only owes to her cultivated art of putting it the distinction enjoyed when some ideal of expression has the *whole* of the case, the case once made its concern, in charge, but might further act for us, were we to follow up her exhibition, as lighting not a little that question of tone, the author's own intrinsic, as to which we have just seen Mr. Conrad's late production rather tend to darken counsel. "The Custom of the Country" is an eminent instance of the sort of tonic value most opposed to that baffled relation between the subject matter and its emergence which we find constituted by the circumvallations of "Chance." Mrs.

Wharton's reaction in presence of the aspects of life hitherto, it would seem, mainly exposed to her is for the most part the ironic; to which we gather these particular aspects to have so much ministered that were we to pursue the quest we might recognise in them precisely the saturation as to which we a moment ago reserved our judgment. "The Custom of the Country" is at any rate consistently, almost scientifically satiric, as indeed the satiric light was doubtless the only one in which the elements could at all be focussed together. But this happens directly to the profit of something that, as we read, becomes more and more one with the principle of authority at work; the light that gathers is a dry light, of great intensity, and the effect, if not rather the very essence, of its dryness is a particular fine asperity. The usual "creative" conditions and associations, as we have elsewhere languished among them, are, thanks to this, ever so sensibly altered; the general authoritative relation attested becomes clear; we move in an air purged at a stroke of the old sentimental and romantic values, the perversions with the maximum of waste of perversions, and we shall not here attempt to state what this makes for in the way of æsthetic refreshment and relief; the waste having kept us so dangling on the dark æsthetic abyss. A shade of asperity may be in such fashion a security against waste, and in the dearth of displayed securities we should welcome it on that ground alone. It helps at any rate to constitute for the talent manifest in "The Custom" a rare

identity, so far should we have to go to seek another instance of the dry, or call it perhaps even the hard, intellectual touch in the soft, or call it perhaps even the
humid, temperamental air; in other words of the masculine conclusion tending so to crown the feminine
observation.

IV

If we mentioned Mr. Compton Mackenzie at the beginning of these reflections only to leave him waiting
for some further appreciation, this is exactly because his
case, to the most interesting effect, is no simple one, like
two or three of our others, but on the contrary mystifying
enough almost to stand by itself. What would be this
striking young writer's state of acquaintance and possession, and should we find it, on our recognition of it, to be
all he is content to pitch forth without discriminations or
determinants, without motives or lights? Do "Carnival"
and "Sinister Street" proceed from the theory of the
slice or from the conception of the extract, "the extract
flasked and fine," the chemical process superseding the
mechanical?

Mr. Compton Mackenzie's literary aspect, though de-
cidedly that of youth, or that of experience, a great deal
of young experience, in its freshness, offers the attraction
of a complexity defiant of the prompt conclusion, really
charms us by giving us something to wonder about. We
literally find it not easy to say if there may not lurk in

o

"Carnival," for example, a selective sense more appre-
hensible to a push of inquiry than its overflooded surface,
a real invitation to wade and upon which everything
within the author's ken appears poured out, would at first
lead us to suspect. The question comes up in like fashion
as to the distinctly more developed successor of that work,
before which we in fact find questions multiply to a
positive quickening of critical pleasure. We ask ourselves what "Sinister Street" may mean as a whole in
spite of our sense of being brushed from the first by a
hundred subordinate purposes, the succession and alter-
nation of which seem to make after a fashion a plan, and
which, though full of occasional design, yet fail to
measure themselves for application or to converge to an
idea. Any idea will serve, ever, that has held up its
candle to composition—and it is perhaps because composition proposes itself under Mr. Compton Mackenzie's
energy on a scale well nigh of the most prodigious that
we must wait to see whither it tends. The question of
what he may here mean "on the whole," as we just said,
is doubtless admonished to stand back till we are possessed of the whole. This interesting volume is but a
first, committed up to its eyes to continuity and with an
announced sequel to follow. The recital exhibits at the
point we have reached the intimate experience of a boy
at school and in his holidays, the amplification of which
is to come with his terms and their breaks at a university;
and the record will probably form a more squared and

extended picture of life equally conditioned by the extremity of youth than we shall know where else to look for.

Youth clearly has been Mr. Mackenzie's saturation, as it has been Mr. Hugh Walpole's; but we see this not as a subject (youth in itself is no specific subject, any more than age is), but as matter for a subject and as requiring a motive to redeem it from the merely passive state of the slice. We are sure throughout both "Sinister Street" and "Carnival" of breathing the air of the extract, as we contentiously call it, only in certain of the rounded episodes strung on the loose cord as so many vivid beads, each of its chosen hue, and the series of which, even with differences of price between them, we take for a lively gage of performance to come. These episodes would be easy to cite; they are handsomely numerous and each strikes us as giving in its turn great salience to its motive. Besides, each is in its turn "done" with an eminent sense and a remarkably straight hand for doing. They may well be cited together as signally and finely symptomatic, for the literary gesture and the bravura breadth with which such frequent medallions as the adventure on the boy's part of the Catholic church at Bournemouth, as his experiment of the Benedictine house in Wiltshire, as his period of acquaintance with the æsthetic *cénacle* in London, as his relation with his chosen school friend under the intensity of boyish choosing are ornamentally hung up, differ not so much in degree as in kind from any play of presentation that we mostly see elsewhere offered us. To which

we might add other like matters that we lack space to
enumerate, the scenes, the aspects, the figure in motion
tending always, under touches thick and strong, to
emerge and flush, sound and strike, catch us in its truth.
We have heard "tales of school life" in which the boys
more or less swarmed and sounded, but from which the
masters have practically been quite absent, to the great
weakening of any picture of the boyish consciousness,
on which the magisterial fact is so heavily projected. If
that is less true for some boys than for others the "point"
of Michael Fane is that for him it is truest. The types of
masters have in "Sinister Street" both number and
salience, rendered though they be mostly as grotesques
—which effect we take as characterizing the particular
turn of mind of the young observer and discoverer
commemorated.

That he *is* a discoverer is of the essence of his interest,
a successful and resourceful young discoverer, even as
the poor ballet-girl in "Carnival" is a tragically baffled
and helpless one; so that what each of the works proposes
to itself is a recital of the things discovered. Those thus
brought to view in the boy's case are of much more
interest, to our sense, than like matters in the other connexion, thanks to his remarkable and living capacity; the
heroine of "Carnival" is frankly too minute a vessel of
experience for treatment on the scale on which the author
has honoured her—she is done assuredly, but under
multiplications of touch that become too much, in the

narrow field, monotonies; and she leaves us asking almost
as much what she exhibitionally means, what application
resides in the accumulation of facts concerning her, as if
she too were after all but a slice, or at the most but a slice
of a slice, and her history but one of the aspects, on her
author's part, of the condition of repleteness against the
postulate of the entire adequacy of which we protest. So
far as this record does affect us as an achieved "extract,"
to reiterate our term, that result abides in its not losing its
centre, which is its fidelity to the one question of her dole-
fully embarrassed little measure of life. We know to that
extent with some intensity what her producer would be
at, yet an element of the arbitrary hangs for us about the
particular illustration—illustrations leaving us ever but
half appreciative till we catch that one bright light in
which they give out all they contain.

This light is of course always for the author to set
somewhere. Is it set then so much as it should be in
"Sinister Street," and is our impression of the promise
of this recital one with a dawning divination of the illustrative card that Mr. Mackenzie may still have up his
sleeve and that our aftersense shall recognise as the last
thing left on the table? By no means, we can as yet easily
say, for if a boy's experience has ever been given us for its
face value simply, for whatever it is worth in more drawn-
out vibration, it is so given us here. Of all the saturations
it can in fact scarce have helped being the most sufficient
in itself, since from beginning to end it is exactly, where

it is best, the recovered and reported thing, that thing alone, that thing existent in the field of memory, though gaining value too from the applied intelligence, or in other words from the lively talent, of the memorizer. The memorizer helps, he contributes, he completes, and what we have admired in him is that in the case of each of the pearls fished up by his dive—though indeed these fruits of the rummage are not all pearls—his mind has had a further iridescence to confer. It is the fineness of the iridescence that on such an occasion matters, and this appeal to our interest is again and again on Mr. Compton Mackenzie's page of the happiest and the brightest. It is never more so than when we catch him, as we repeatedly do, in the act of positively caring for his expression as expression, positively providing for his phrase as a fondly foreseeing parent for a child, positively loving it in the light of what it may do for him—meeting revelations, that is, in what it may do, and appearing to recognise that the value of the offered thing, its whole relation to us, is created by the breath of language, that on such terms exclusively, for appropriation and enjoyment, we know it, and that any claimed independence of "form" on its part is the most abject of fallacies. Do these things mean that, moved by life, this interesting young novelist is even now uncontrollably on the way to style? We might cite had we space several symptoms, the very vividest, of that possibility; though such an appearance in the field of our general survey has against it presumptions enough to bring us surely back to our original contention—the scant degree in which that field has ever had to reckon with criticism.

66

H. G. WELLS

"Digression about Novels" [1]

I FIND before me a considerable accumulation of material, first assembled together in a folder labelled "Whether I am a Novelist." It has been extremely difficult to digest this material into a presentable form. It refuses to be simplified. It is like a mental shunting yard in which several trains of thought have come into collision and I feel now that the utmost I can do with it is not so much to set these trains going again as to salvage some few fragmentary observations from the wreckage.

One of these trains comes in from the previous section. It is an insistence upon the importance of individuality and individual adjustment in life; "Problems of association between men and women and an infinitude of opportunities for mutual charity." That carries on very obviously towards the idea of the novel as an expanding discussion of "How did they treat each other? How might they have treated each other? How should they

---

[1] *Experiment in Autobiography*, pp. 487–504.

treat each other?" I set out to write novels, as distinguished from those pseudo-scientific stories in which imaginative experience rather than personal conduct was the matter in hand, on the assumption that problems of adjustment were the essential matter for novel-writing. *Love and Mr. Lewisham* was entirely a story about a dislocation and an adjustment.

But across the track of that train of thought came another in which the novel presented itself not as an ethical enquiry but as the rendering of a system of impressions. In this distended and irregularly interesting folder, which I find so hard to reduce to straightforward explicitness, I find myself worrying round various talks and discussions I had with Henry James a third of a century ago. He was a very important figure in the literary world of that time and a shrewd and penetrating critic of the technique by which he lived. He liked me and he found my work respectable enough to be greatly distressed about it. I bothered him and he bothered me. We were at cross purposes based as I shall show later on very fundamental differences, not only of temperament but training. He had no idea of the possible use of the novel as a help to conduct. His mind has turned away from any such idea. From his point of view there were not so much "novels" as The Novel, and it was a very high and important achievement. He thought of it as an Art Form and of novelists as artists of a very special and exalted type. He was concerned about their greatness and repute. He saw us all as Masters or would-be Masters, little Masters and great Masters, and he was plainly sorry that "Cher Maître" was not an English expression. One could not be in a room with him for ten minutes without realizing the importance he attached to the dignity of this art of his. I was by nature and education unsympathetic with this mental disposition. But I was disposed to regard a novel as about as much an art form as a market place or a boulevard. It had not even necessarily to get anywhere. You went by it on your various occasions.

That was entirely out of key with James's assumptions. I recall a talk I had with him soon after the publication of *Marriage*. With tact and circumlocution, James broke it to me, that he found a remarkable deficiency in that story. It was a deficiency that he had also observed in a vast proportion of contemporary fiction, it had exercised him very fruitfully, and his illuminating comments spread out from that starting point to a far-reaching tentacular discussion of what a novel should do and be.

The point he was stressing was this: *Marriage* is the story of a young man of science, Trafford, who, apparently without much previous experience, pilots a friend's aeroplane (in 1912!) and crashes, he and the friend together, into a croquet party and the Pope family and the life of Marjorie Pope. Thereupon there is bandaging, ambulance work and much coming and going and Marjorie, who is already engaged to a Mr. Magnet, falls deeply in love with Trafford. She drives to the village in a donkey cart to do some shopping and meets the lamed Trafford, also driving a donkey cart and their wheels interlock and they fall talking. All that—except for the writing of it—was tolerable according to James. But then, in order to avoid the traffic in the high road the two young people take their respective donkey carts into a side lane and remain there talking for three hours. And this is where James's objection came in. Of the three hours of intercourse in the lane the novel tells nothing, except that the young people emerged in open and declared love with each other. This, said James, wasn't playing the game. I had cut out an essential, after a feast of irrelevant particulars. Gently but firmly he insisted that I did not myself know what had happened and what was said in that lane; that there was even a touch of improbability about their staying there so long and that this lack of information and probability at a crucial point was due to the fact that I had not thought out the individualities concerned with sufficient care and thoroughness. I had not cared enough about these individualities. Moreover in the conversations between the two principals, the man in particular supplied information about himself and his position in life in such a way as to talk at the reader instead of to the girl. The talk was in fact more for the benefit of the former. Trafford had to supply this information because I had been too inept or hasty to convey it in any other way. Or because there was too much to convey in any other way. Henry James was quite right in saying that I had not thought out these two people to the pitch of saturation and that they did not behave unconsciously and naturally. But my defence is that that did not matter, or at least that for the purposes of the book it did not matter very much.[1]

Now I do not exactly remember the several other points he made in that elaborate critical excursion, nor did I attempt any reprisals upon his own work, but his gist was plain. If the Novel was properly a presentation of real people as real people, in absolutely natural reaction in a story, then my characters were not simply sketchy, they were eked out by wires and pads of non-living matter and they stood condemned. His discourse, which had evidently been maturing against my visit, covered not only my work but that of several of my contemporaries whom he had also read with interest and distaste. And the only point upon which I might have argued but which I did not then argue, was this, that the Novel was not necessarily, as he assumed, this real through and through and absolutely true treatment of people more living than life. It might be more and less than that and still be a novel.

To illustrate with what lovely complication of veracity and disingenuousness, with what curious intricate suavity of intimation he could develop his point I will quote from a letter of his, also bearing upon the same book *Marriage*. His intricate mind, as persistent and edentate as a pseudopodium, was still worrying round and about the question

[1] See pp. 190–91 for James's published discussion of *Marriage*.

raised by that story. [Wells here quotes most of James's letter to him of 18th October 1912.]

Tried by Henry James's standards I doubt if any of my novels can be taken in any other fashion. There are flashes and veins of character duly "treated" and living individuals in many of them, but none that satisfy his requirements fully. A lot of *Kipps* may pass, some of *Tono-Bungay*, *Mr. Britling Sees it Through* and *Joan and Peter* and let me add, I have a weakness for Lady Harman and for Theodore Bulpington and——. But I will not run on. These are pleas in extenuation. The main indictment is sound, that I sketch out scenes and individuals, often quite crudely, and resort even to conventional types and symbols, in order to get on to a discussion of relationships. The important point which I tried to argue with Henry James was that the novel of completely consistent characterization arranged beautifully in a story and painted deep and round and solid, no more exhausts the possibilities of the novel, than the art of Velazquez exhausts the possibilities of the painted picture.

The issue exercised my mind considerably. I had a queer feeling that we were both incompatably right. I wrote one or two lectures and critical papers on the scope of the novel, and I argued with myself and others, that realism and exhaustive presentation were not its only objectives. I think I might have gone further and maintained that they were not even its proper objectives but at best only graces by the way, but at the time I was not clear enough to say that. I might have made a good case by asserting that fiction was necessarily fictitious through and through, and that the real analogy to Velazquez who painted straight from dwarfs and kings, would be biography, character drawn straight from life and not an invented story. James was very much against the idea that there was a biographical element in any good novel, and he and his brother William were very severe upon Vernon Lee when she produced a character in a short story (*Lady Tal*, 1892) markedly like Henry. But it is beyond the power of man to "create" individuals absolutely. If we do not write from models then we compile and fabricate. Every "living" character in a novel is drawn, frankly or furtively, from life—is filched from biography whole or in scraps, a portrait or a patch-up, and its actions are a reflection upon moral conduct. At whatever number of "removes" from facts we may be, we are still imputing motives to somebody. That is the conclusion I am coming to now, but I did not have it ready at that time. I allowed it to be taken for granted that there was such a thing as The Novel, a great and stately addendum to reality, a sort of super-reality with "created" persons in it, and by implication I admitted that my so-called novels were artless self-revelatory stuff, falling far away from a stately ideal by which they had to be judged.

But now I ask when and where has that great ideal been realized—or can it ever be realized?

Competent critics have since examined this supreme importance of individualities, in other words of "character" in the fiction of the nineteenth century and early twentieth century. Throughout that period character-interest did its best to take the place of adjustment-interest in fiction. With a certain justice these authorities ascribe the predominance of individuation to the example of Sir Walter Scott. But more generally it was a consequence of the prevalent sense of social stability, and he was not so much a primary influence as an exponent. He was a man of intensely conservative quality; he accepted, he accepted wilfully, the established social values about him; he had hardly a doubt in him of what was right or wrong, handsome or ungracious, just or mean. He saw events therefore as a play of individualities in a rigid frame of values never more to be questioned or permanently changed. His lawless, romantic past was the picturesque prelude to stability; our current values were already potentially there. Throughout the broad smooth flow of nineteenth-century life in Great Britain, the art of fiction floated on this same assumption of social fixity. The Novel in English was produced in an atmosphere of security for the entertainment of secure people who liked to feel established and safe for good. Its standards were established within that apparently permanent frame and the criticism of it began to be irritated and perplexed when, through a new instability, the splintering frame began to get into the picture.

I suppose for a time I was the outstanding instance among writers of fiction in English of the frame getting into the picture.

I did not see this clearly in those opening years of this century, but in 1912 I made a sort of pronouncement against the "character" obsession and the refusal to discuss values, in a paper on "The Contemporary Novel" delivered to the Times Book Club, in which I argued for an enlarging scope for the novel. My attack upon the creation-of-character idea was oblique and subconscious rather than direct. [Wells here quotes the last few sentences of "The Contemporary Novel."]

These are brave trumpetings. In effect in my hands the Novel proved like a blanket too small for the bed and when I tried to pull it over to cover my tossing conflict of ideas, I found I had to abandon questions of individuation. I never got "all life within the scope of the novel." (What a phrase! Who could?)

In the criticism of that time there was a certain confusion between this new spreading out of the interest of the novel to issues of custom and political and social change, and the entirely more limited "Novel with a Purpose" of the earlier nineteenth century. This examined no essential ideas; its values were established values, it merely assailed some particular evil, exposed some little-known abuse. It kept well within the frame. The majority of the Dickens novels were novels with a purpose, but they never deal with any inner confusion, any conflicts of opinion within the individual characters, any subjective essential change. A much closer approximation to the spread-out novel I was advocating is the propaganda novel. But I have always resented having my novels called propaganda novels, because it seems to me the word propaganda should be confined to the definite service of some organized party, church or doctrine. It implies direction from outside. If at times I have been inclined to thrust views upon my readers, they were at any rate my own views and put forward without any strategic aim.

To return to this novel *Marriage*, the story tells how masculine intellectual interest met feminine spending and what ensued. Trafford is not so much a solid man as a scientific intelligence caught in the meshes of love, and Marjorie Pope's zest in buying and arrangement is emphasized to the exclusion of any minor tricks and turns. But the argument of the book would not have stood out, if there had been any such tricks and turns. Marjorie's father is an intrusion of character drawing who really had no business in the book at all. Mr. Magnet also is a slightly malicious irrelevance; the humourless speech he makes in London on humour is, for example, transcribed verbatim from a reported speech by a distinguished contemporary.

Indisputably the writing is scamped in places. It could have been just as light and much better done. But that would have taken more time than I could afford. I do not mean by that I could have earned less money and been a more conscientious writer, though that consideration very probably came in, but I mean that I had very many things to say and that if I could say one of them in such a way as to get my point over to the reader I did not worry much about finish. The fastidious critic might object, but the general reader to whom I addressed myself cared no more for finish and fundamental veracity about the secondary things of behaviour than I. I did not want to sweep under the mat for crumbs of characterization, nor did he want me to do so. What we wanted was a ventilation of the point at issue.

It required some years and a number of such experiments and essays in statement as the one I have quoted, before I got it really clear in my own mind that I was feeling my way towards something outside any established formula for the novel altogether. In the established novel, objective through and through, the characteristic exterior reactions of the character were everything and the conflicts and changes of ideas within his brain were ignored. (That according to the jargon of the time would have been to "introduce controversial matter.") But I was becoming more and more interested in the interior conflict, this controversial matter stewing and fermenting in all our brains, and its ventilation in action. There is no satisfactory device I knew for exhibiting a train of reasoning in a character unless a set of ideas similar to those upon which the character thinks exists

P

already in the reader's mind. Galsworthy's Soames Forsyte *thinks* for pages, but he thinks along recognized British lines. He does not grapple with ideas new and difficult both for the reader and himself. I could not see how, if we were to grapple with new ideas, a sort of argument with the reader, an explanation of the theory that is being exhibited, could be avoided. I began therefore to make my character indulge in impossibly explicit monologues and duologues. As early as 1902, Chatteris in the *Sea Lady* talks a good deal more than is natural. *Ann Veronica* soliloquizes continually. In *Marriage* (1912), Trafford and Marjorie go off to Labrador for a good honest six months talk about their mutual reactions and argue at the reader all the time. Mr. Brumley in *The Wife of Sir Isaac Harman* (1914) exercises a garrulous pressure upon the flow of the story throughout. *The Research Magnificent* (1915) is largely talk and monologue. I try in that book the device of making the ostensible writer speculate about the chief character in the story he is telling. The ostensible writer becomes a sort of enveloping character, himself in discussion with the reader. Still more expository is the *Soul of a Bishop* (1917).

Incidentally I may complain that *The Research Magnificent* is a book deserving to be remembered and yet seems to be largely forgotten. I liked it when I re-read it and I find it remarkably up to date with my present opinions. It was blotted out by the war. But Amanda is alive and Benham has his moments of vitality.

By 1919, in *The Undying Fire*, I was at last fully aware of what I was doing and I took a new line. I realized I had been trying to revive the Dialogue in a narrative form. I was not so much expanding the novel as getting right out of it. *The Undying Fire* is that great Hebrew imitation of the Platonic Dialogue, the Book of Job, frankly modernized. The arrangement of the ancient book is followed very closely; the speakers even to their names are recognizably the same. The man of Uz is Mr. Job Huss; Eliphaz the Temanite becomes Sir Eliphaz Burrows, manufacturer of a new building material called Temanite, Bildad is Mr. William Dad and Elihu becomes Dr. Elihu Barrack. They parallel their ancient arguments; even their speeches in their order correspond closely with the pattern of the ancient book. In many ways I think *The Undying Fire* one of the best pieces of work I ever did. I set great store by it still.

But after all these protests of the excellence and intelligence of my intentions, I have to admit that the larger part of my fiction was written lightly and with a certain haste. Only one or two of my novels deal primarily with personality, and then rather in the spirit of what David Low calls the caricature-portrait, than for the purpose of such exhaustive rendering as Henry James had in mind. Such caricature-individualities are Hoopdriver in *The Wheels of Chance* (1896), *Kipps* (1905) and Mr. Polly in *The History of Mr. Polly* (1910). My uncle and aunt in *Tono-Bungay* (1909), one or two minor characters in *The Dream* (1924), *Christina Alberta's Father* (1925) and *The Bulpington of Blup* (1932), are also caricature-individualities of which I am not ashamed. Theodore Bulpington is as good as Kipps. Please. But I doubt if any of these persons have that sort of vitality which endures into new social phases. In the course of a few decades they may become incomprehensible; the snobbery of Kipps for example or the bookish illiteracy of Mr. Polly may be altogether inexplicable. *The Dream* is an attempt to show how our lives to-day may look to our happier descendants. It is in the same class as *In the Days of the Comet*.

My experimentation with what I may call the Dialogue Novel was only one of the directions in which I have wandered away from the uncongenial limitations of the novel proper. The plain fact is that I have never been willing to respect these limitations or to accept the Novel as an art form. *Mr. Britling Sees it Through* is a circumstantial story, but it ends in Dialogue and Monologue. *Joan and Peter* (1918) again starts respectably in large novel form and becomes dialogue only towards the end. It is as shamelessly unfinished as a Gothic cathedral. It was to have been a great novel about Education but it grew so large that Peter's public-school experiences, among other things, had to be left out. He just jumps from the preparatory school to the War and the flying corps. The missing public-school stage is to be found in *The Story of a Great Schoolmaster*. Joan I like as a character; A. A. Milne has said nice things about her, but nobody else has had a good word for her—or indeed a bad one. *The Dream* (1924) has some good minor characters, but it is plainly a social criticism from a new angle, rather than a novel proper. A young man of the great world of the future on a holiday walk in the mountains, injures his hand, falls into a fever and dreams "through a whole life" of our present world. *The World of William Clissold* (1926) again is quite unorthodox in shape and approach. It is an attempt to present a thesis upon contemporary life and social development, in the form of a fictitious autobiography. A young chemist, like Trafford in *Marriage*, gives up pure research for industrial organization, grows rich, finds his successful life boring and retires to a house in Provence to think things out and find a better use for himself. He writes the one book that every man has it in him to write. The main strand of the earlier novels reappears in this, the perplexity of the man with general ideas and a strong constructive impulse when he finds that the women he meets do not enter into this stream of motive, but, except for the odd concluding "book," this obsession of so much of my fiction sits lightly here because of the predominance of economic and political questioning. . . .

The Autocracy of Mr. Parham (1930) is a rather boisterous caricature not of the personality but of the imaginations of a modern British imperialist of the university type. It might have been dedicated to Mr. L. S.

Amery. It amuses me still, but few people share my liking. Reality has outdone fiction since and Mosley fooling it in the Albert Hall with his black shirts (1934) makes Parham's great dream-meeting there seem preposterously sane and sound. *Men Like Gods* frankly caricatures some prominent contemporaries. Another breach of established literary standards with which, in spite of its very tepid reception, I am mainly content, was *Mr. Blettsworthy on Rampole Island* (1928). I laughed when writing both it and *Men Like Gods* and *The Autocracy of Mr. Parham*. The gist of Rampole Island is a caricature-portrait of the whole human world. I wish I could hear at times of people still reading these three stories. They got, I think, a dull press.

Exhaustive character study is an adult occupation, a philosophical occupation. So much of my life has been a prolonged and enlarged adolescence, an encounter with the world in general, that the observation of character began to play a leading part in it only in my later years. It was necessary for me to reconstruct the frame in which individual lives as a whole had to be lived, before I could concentrate upon any of the individual problems of fitting them into this frame. I am taking more interest now in individuality than ever I did before. As mankind settles down into the security of that modern world-state with which contemporary life is in labour, as men's minds escape more and more from the harsh urgencies and feelings of a primary struggle, as the conception of the modern world-state becomes the common basis of their education and the frame of their conduct, the discussion of primary issues will abate and the analysis of individual difference again become a dominating interest. But then surely people will be less round-about in their approach to expression and the subterfuge of fiction will not be so imperative as it is to-day.

Our restraints upon the written discussion of living people are antiquated. Why should David Low say practically what he likes about actual people with his pencil, while I must declare every character in a novel is fictitious? So I am disposed to question whether the Novel will have any great importance in the intellectual life of the future because I believe we are moving towards a greater freedom of truthful comment upon individuals; if it survives I think it will become more frankly caricature-comment upon personalities and social phases than it is at present, but it seems equally probable to me that it will dwindle and die altogether and be replaced by more searching and outspoken biography and autobiography. Stories, parables, parodies of fact will still be told, but that is a different matter. The race of silly young men who announce that they are going to write The Novel may follow the race of silly young men who used to proclaim their intention of writing The Epic, to limbo. In my time The Novel, as projected, was usually a "Trilogy." Perhaps in 1965 the foolish young man will all be trailing in the wake of Lytton Strachey and Philip

Guedalla and announcing colossal biography-sequences. They will produce vast mosaics of pseudo-reality, galleries of portraits, presenting contemporary history in a state of exaltation.

Who would read a novel if we were permitted to write biography—all out? Here in this autobiography I am experimenting—though still very mildly, with biographical and auto-biographical matter. Although it has many restraints, which are from the artistic point of view vexatious, I still find it so much more real and interesting and satisfying that I doubt if I shall ever again turn back towards The Novel. I may write a story or so more—a dialogue, an adventure or an anecdote. But I shall never come as near to a deliberate attempt upon The Novel again as I did in *Tono-Bungay* (1909).

Next to *Tono-Bungay*, *Mr. Britling Sees it Through* and *Joan and Peter* come as near to being full-dress novels as anything I have written. They are both fairly sound pictures of contemporary conditions. *Mr. Britling Sees it Through* was a huge success more particularly in America, where it earned about £20,000; *Tono-Bungay* did well; but *Joan and Peter* never won the recognition I think it deserved. To me it seems a far finer piece of work than *Mr. Britling Sees it Through*.

Even *Tono-Bungay* was not much of a concession to Henry James and his conception of an intensified rendering of feeling and characterization as the proper business of the novelist. It was an indisputable Novel, but it was extensive rather than intensive. That is to say it presented characters only as part of a *scene*. It was planned as a social panorama in the vein of Balzac. That vein has produced some physically and mentally great books, and it continues to this day to produce evidences of the nervous endurance of ambitious writers, vast canvasses, too often crude or conventional in interpretation, superficial in motivation and smeary and wholesale in treatment. I cannot imagine it holding out against a literature of competent historical and contemporary studies. *The Forsyte Saga*, as a broadly conceived picture of prosperous British Philistia by one of its indigenes, is not so good and convincing as a group of untrammelled biographical studies of genteel successful types, might be. An industrious treatment of early nineteenth century records again would make Balzac's *Comédie Humaine* seem flighty stuff. Yet in *War and Peace* one may perhaps find a justification for the enhancement and animation of history by fictitious moods and scenes. . . .

67

H. G. WELLS

"Of Art, of Literature, of Mr. Henry James"[1]

§ 1

THE Garden by the Sea chapter was to have gone on discursively with a discussion upon this project of a conference upon the Mind of the Race. The automobileful of gentlemen who had first arrived was to have supplied the opening interlocutors, but presently they were to have been supplemented by the most unexpected accessories. It would have been an enormously big dialogue if it had ever been written, and Boon's essentially lazy temperament was all against its ever getting written. There were to have been disputes from the outset as to the very purpose that had brought them all together. "A sort of literary stocktaking" was to have been Mr. Archer's phrase. Repeated. Unhappily, its commercialism was to upset Mr. Gosse extremely; he was to say something passionately bitter about its "utter lack of dignity." Then relenting a little, he was to urge as an alternative "some controlling influence, some standard and restraint, a new and better Academic influence." Dr. Keyhole was to offer his journalistic services in organiz-

---

[1] *Boon, The Mind of the Race, The Wild Asses of the Devil*, and *The Last Trump* (London, 1915), pp. 84–128.

ing an Academic plebiscite, a suggestion which was to have exasperated Mr. Gosse to the pitch of a gleaming silence.

In the midst of this conversation the party is joined by Hallery and an American friend, a quiet Harvard sort of man speaking meticulously accurate English, and still later by emissaries of Lord Northcliffe and Mr. Hearst, by Mr. Henry James, rather led into it by a distinguished hostess, by Mr. W. B. Yeats, late but keen, and by that Sir Henry Lunn who organizes the Swiss winter sports hotels. All these people drift in with an all too manifestly simulated accidentalness that at last arouses the distrust of the elderly custodian, so that Mr. Orage, the gifted editor of the *New Age*, arriving last, is refused admission. The sounds of the conflict at the gates do but faintly perturb the conference within, which is now really getting to business, but afterwards Mr. Orage, slightly wounded in the face by a dexterously plied rake and incurably embittered, makes his existence felt by a number of unpleasant missiles discharged from over the wall in the direction of any audible voices. Ultimately Mr. Orage gets into a point of vantage in a small pine-tree overlooking the seaward corner of the premises, and from this he contributes a number of comments that are rarely helpful, always unamiable, and frequently in the worst possible taste.

Such was Boon's plan for the second chapter of "The Mind of the Race." But that chapter he never completely planned. At various times Boon gave us a number of colloquies, never joining them together in any regular order. The project of taking up the discussion of the Mind of the Race at the exact point Mr. Mallock had laid it down, and taking the villa by the sea for the meeting-place, was at once opposed by Hallery and his American friend with an evidently preconcerted readiness. They pointed out the entire democratization of thought and literature that had been going on for the past four decades. It was no longer possible to deal with such matters in the old aristocratic country-house style; it was no longer possible to take them up from that sort of beginning; the centre of mental gravity among the English-speaking community had shifted socially and geographically; what was needed now was something wider and ampler, something more in the nature of such a conference as the annual meeting of the British Association. Science left the gentleman's mansion long ago; literature must follow it—had followed it. To come back to Mr. Lankester's Villa by the sea was to come back to a beaten covert. The Hearst representative took up a strongly supporting position, and suggested that if indeed we wished to move with the times the thing to do was to strike out boldly for a special annex of the Panama Exhibition at San Francisco and for organization upon sound American lines. It was a case, he said, even for "exhibits." Sir Henry Lunn, however, objected that in America the Anglo-Saxon note was almost certain to be too exclusively sounded; that

we had to remember there were vigorous cultures growing up and growing up more and more detachedly upon
the continent of Europe; we wanted, at least, their reflected lights . . . some more central position . . . In fact,
Switzerland . . . where also numerous convenient hotels
. . . patronized, he gathered from the illustrated papers,
by Lord Lytton, Mrs. Asquith, Mr. F. R. Benson . . .
and all sorts of helpful leading people.

§ 2

MEANWHILE Boon's plan was to make Mr. George Moore
and Mr. Henry James wander off from the general dispute, and he invented a dialogue that even at the time
struck me as improbable, in which both gentlemen pursue entirely independent trains of thought.

Mr. Moore's conception of the projected symposium
was something rather in the vein of the journeyings of
Shelley, Byron, and their charming companions through
France to Italy, but magnified to the dimensions of an
enormous pilgrimage, enlarged to the scale of a stream
of refugees. "What, my dear James," he asked, "is this
mind of humanity at all without a certain touch of
romance, of adventure? Even Mallock appreciated the
significance of *frou-frou*; but these fellows behind
here . . ."

To illustrate his meaning better, he was to have told,
with an extraordinary and loving mastery of detail, of a
glowing little experience that had been almost forced

upon him at Nismes by a pretty little woman from Nebraska, and the peculiar effect it had had, and particularly
the peculiar effect that the coincidence that both Nebraska
and Nismes begin with an "N" and end so very differ-
ently, had had upon his imagination. . . .

Meanwhile Mr. James, being anxious not merely to
state but also to ignore, laboured through the long
cadences of his companion as an indefatigable steam-tug
might labour endlessly against a rolling sea, elaborat-
ing his own particular point about the proposed conference.

"Owing it as we do," he said, "very, very largely to
our friend Gosse, to that peculiar, that honest but restless
and, as it were, at times almost malignantly ambitious
organizing energy of our friend, I cannot altogether—
altogether, even if in any case I should have taken so
extreme, so devastatingly isolating a step as, to put it
violently, *stand out*; yet I must confess to a considerable
anxiety, a kind of distress, an apprehension, the terror,
so to speak, of the kerbstone, at all this stream of intellectual trafficking, of going to and fro, in a superb and
towering manner enough no doubt, but still essentially
going to and fro rather than in any of the completed
senses of the word *getting there*, that does so largely constitute the aggregations and activities we are invited to
traverse. My poor head, such as it is and as much as it can
and upon such legs—save the mark!—as it can claim,
must, I suppose, play its inconsiderable part among the

wheels and the rearings and the toots and the whistles and all this uproar, this—Mm, Mm!—let us say, this *infernal* uproar, of the occasion; and if at times one has one's doubts before plunging in, whether after all, after the plunging and the dodging and the close shaves and narrow squeaks, one does begin to feel that one is getting through, whether after all one *will* get through, and whether indeed there is any getting through, whether, to deepen and enlarge and display one's doubt quite openly, there is in truth any sort of ostensible and recognizable other side attainable and definable at all, whether to put this thing with a lucidity that verges on the brutal, whether our amiable and in most respects our adorable Gosse isn't indeed preparing here and now, not the gathering together of a conference but the assembling, the *meet*, so to speak, of a wild-goose chase of an entirely desperate and hopeless description."

At that moment Mr. George Moore was saying: "Little exquisite shoulders without a touch of colour and with just that suggestion of rare old ivory in an old shop window in some out-of-the-way corner of Paris that only the most patent abstinence from baths and the brutality of soaping——"

Each gentleman stopped simultaneously.

Ahead the path led between box-hedges to a wall, and above the wall was a pine-tree, and the Editor of the *New Age* was re-ascending the pine-tree in a laborious and resolute manner, gripping with some difficulty in his

hand a large and very formidable lump of unpleasant-
ness. . . .

With a common impulse the two gentlemen turned
back towards the house.

Mr. James was the first to break the momentary
silence. "And so, my dear Moore, and so—to put it
shortly—without any sort of positive engagement or
entanglement or pledge or pressure—I *came*. And at the
proper time and again with an entirely individual detachment and as little implication as possible I shall *go*. . . ."

Subsequently Mr. James was to have buttonholed
Hallery's American, and in the warm bath of his sympathy to have opened and bled slowly from another vein
of thought.

"I admit the abundance of—what shall I say?—
activities that our friend is summoning, the tremendous
wealth of matter, of material for literature and art, that
has accumulated during the last few decades. No one
could appreciate, could savour and watch and respond,
more than myself to the tremendous growing clangour of
the mental process as the last half-century has exhibited
it. But when it comes to the enterprise of gathering it together, and not simply just gathering it together, but
gathering it *all* together, then surely one must at some stage
ask the question, *Why* all? Why, in short, attempt to a com-
prehensiveness that must be overwhelming when in fact
the need is for a selection that shall not merely represent
but elucidate and lead. Aren't we, after all, all of us after

some such indicating projection of a leading digit, after such an insistence on the outstandingly essential in face of this abundance, this saturation, this fluid chaos that perpetually increases? Here we are gathering together to celebrate and summarize literature in some sort of undefined and unprecedented fashion, and for the life of me I find it impossible to determine what among my numerous associates and friends and—to embrace still larger quantities of the stuff in hand—my contemporaries is considered to be the literature in question. So confused now are we between matter and treatment, between what is stated and documented and what is prepared and presented, that for the life of me I do not yet see whether we are supposed to be building an ark or whether by immersion and the meekest of submersions and an altogether complete submission of our distended and quite helpless carcasses to its incalculable caprice we are supposed to be celebrating and, in the whirling uncomfortable fashion of flotsam at large, indicating and making visible the whole tremendous cosmic inundation. . . ."

§ 3

IT was entirely in the quality of Boon's intellectual untidiness that for a time he should go off at a tangent in pursuit of Mr. Henry James and leave his literary picnic disseminated about the grounds of Mr. Mallock's villa. There, indeed, they remained. The story when he took it up again picked up at quite a different point.

Q

I remember how Boon sat on the wall of his vegetable garden and discoursed upon James, while several of us squatted about on the cucumber-frames and big flower-pots and suchlike seats, and how over the wall Ford Madox Hueffer was beating Wilkins at Badminton. Hueffer wanted to come and talk too; James is one of his countless subjects—and what an omniscient man he is too!—but Wilkins was too cross to let him off. . . .

So that all that Hueffer was able to contribute was an exhortation not to forget that Henry James knew Turgenev and that he had known them both, and a flat denial that Dickens was a novelist. This last was the tail of that Pre-Raphaelite feud begun in *Household Words*, oh! generations ago. . . .

"Got you there, my boy!" said Wilkins. "Seven, twelve."

We heard no more from Hueffer.

"You see," Boon said, "you can't now talk of literature without going through James. James is unavoidable. James is to criticism what Immanuel Kant is to philosophy—a partially comprehensible essential, an inevitable introduction. If you understand what James is up to and if you understand what James is not up to, then you are placed. You are in the middle of the critical arena. You are in a position to lay about you with significance. Otherwise. . . .

"I want to get this Hallery of mine, who is to be the hero of 'The Mind of the Race,' into a discussion with

Henry James, but that, you know, is easier said than imagined. Hallery is to be one of those enthusiastic thinkers who emit highly concentrated opinions in gobbets, suddenly. James—isn't. . . ."

Boon meditated upon his difficulties. "Hallery's idea of literature is something tremendously comprehensive, something that pierces always down towards the core of things, something that carries and changes all the activities of the race. This sort of thing."

He read from a scrap of paper—

" 'The thought of a community is the life of that community, and if the collective thought of a community is disconnected and fragmentary, then the community is collectively vain and weak. That does not constitute an incidental defect but essential failure. Though that community have cities such as the world has never seen before, fleets and hosts and glories, though it count its soldiers by the army corps and its children by the million, yet if it hold not to the reality of thought and formulated will beneath these outward things, it will pass, and all its glories will pass, like smoke before the wind, like mist beneath the sun; it will become at last only one more vague and fading dream upon the scroll of time, a heap of mounds and pointless history, even as are Babylon and Nineveh.' "

"I've heard that before somewhere," said Dodd.

"Most of this dialogue will have to be quotation," said Boon.

"He makes literature include philosophy?"

"Everything. It's all the central things. It's the larger Bible to him, a thing about which all the conscious direction of life revolves. It's alive with passion and will. Or if it isn't, then it ought to be. . . . And then as the antagonist comes this artist, this man who seems to regard the whole seething brew of life as a vat from which you skim, with slow, dignified gestures, works of art. . . . Works of art whose only claim is their art. . . . Hallery is going to be very impatient about art."

"Ought there to be such a thing as a literary artist?" some one said.

"Ought there, in fact, to be Henry James?" said Dodd.

"I don't think so. Hallery won't think so. You see, the discussion will be very fundamental. There's contributory art, of course, and a way of doing things better or worse. Just as there is in war, or cooking. But the way of doing isn't the end. First the end must be judged— and then if you like talk of how it is done. Get there as splendidly as possible. But get there. James and George Moore, neither of them take it like that. They leave out getting there, or the thing they get to is so trivial as to amount to scarcely more than an omission. . . ."

Boon reflected. "In early life both these men poisoned their minds in studios. Thought about pictures even might be less studio-ridden than it is. But James has never discovered that a novel isn't a picture. . . . That life isn't a studio. . . .

"He wants a novel to be simply and completely *done*. He wants it to have a unity, he demands homogeneity. . . . Why *should* a book have that? For a picture it's reasonable, because you have to see it all at once. But there's no need to see a book all at once. It's like wanting to have a whole county done in one style and period of architecture. It's like insisting that a walking tour must stick to one valley. . . .

"But James *begins* by taking it for granted that a novel is a work of art that must be judged by its oneness. Judged first by its oneness. Some one gave him that idea in the beginning of things and he has never found it out. He doesn't find things out. He doesn't even seem to want to find things out. You can see that in him; he is eager to accept things—elaborately. You can see from his books that he accepts etiquettes, precedences, associations, claims. That is his peculiarity. He accepts very readily and then—elaborates. He has, I am convinced, one of the strongest, most abundant minds alive in the whole world, and he has the smallest penetration. Indeed, he has no penetration. He is the culmination of the Superficial type. Or else he would have gone into philosophy and been greater even than his wonderful brother. . . . But here he is, spinning about, like the most tremendous of water-boatmen—you know those insects?—kept up by surface tension. As if, when once he pierced the surface, he would drown. It's incredible. A water-boatman as big as an elephant. I was reading him only yesterday—'The Golden Bowl'; it's dazzling how never for a moment does he go through."

"Recently he's been explaining himself," said Dodd.

"His 'Notes on Novelists.' It's one sustained demand for the picture effect. Which is the denial of the sweet complexity of life, of the pointing this way and that, of the spider on the throne. Philosophy aims at a unity and never gets there. . . . That true unity which we all suspect, and which no one attains, if it is to be got at all it is to be got by penetrating, penetrating down and through. The picture, on the other hand, is forced to a unity because it can see only one aspect at a time. I am doubtful even about that. Think of Hogarth or Carpaccio. But if the novel is to follow life it must be various and discursive. Life is diversity and entertainment, not completeness and satisfaction. All actions are half-hearted, shot delightfully with wandering thoughts—about something else. All true stories are a felt of irrelevances. But James sets out to make his novels with the presupposition that they can be made continuously relevant. And perceiving the discordant things, he tries to get rid of them. He sets himself to pick the straws out of the hair of Life before he paints her. But without the straws she is no longer the mad woman we love. He talks of 'selection,' and of making all of a novel definitely *about* a theme. He objects to a 'saturation' that isn't oriented. And he objects, if you go into it, for no clear reason at all. Following up his conception of selection, see what in his own practice

he omits. In practice James's selection becomes just
omission and nothing more. He omits everything that
demands digressive treatment or collateral statement.
For example, he omits opinions. In all his novels you
will find no people with defined political opinions, no
people with religious opinions, none with clear partisan-
ships or with lusts or whims, none definitely up to any
specific impersonal thing. There are no poor people
dominated by the imperatives of Saturday night and Monday morning, no dreaming types—and don't we all more
or less live dreaming? And none are ever decently for-
getful. All that much of humanity he clears out before he
begins his story. It's like cleaning rabbits for the table.

"But you see how relentlessly it follows from the sup-
position that the novel is a work of art aiming at pictorial
unities!

"All art too acutely self-centred comes to this sort of
thing. James's denatured people are only the equivalent
in fiction of those egg-faced, black-haired ladies, who sit
and sit, in the Japanese colour-prints, the unresisting
stuff for an arrangement of blacks. . . .

"Then with the eviscerated people he has invented he
begins to make up stories. What stories they are! Concentrated on suspicion, on a gift, on possessing a 'piece'
of old furniture, on what a little girl may or may not have
noted in an emotional situation. These people cleared for
artistic treatment never make lusty love, never go to
angry war, never shout at an election or perspire at

poker; never in any way *date*. . . . And upon the petty residuum of human interest left to them they focus minds of a Jamesian calibre. . . .

"The only living human motives left in the novels of Henry James are a certain avidity and an entirely superficial curiosity. Even when relations are irregular or when sins are hinted at, you feel that these are merely attitudes taken up, gambits before the game of attainment and over-perception begins. . . . His people nose out suspicions, hint by hint, link by link. Have you ever known living human beings do that? The thing his novel is *about* is always there. It is like a church lit but without a congregation to distract you, with every light and line focused on the high altar. And on the altar, very reverently placed, intensely there, is a dead kitten, an egg-shell, a bit of string. . . . Like his 'Altar of the Dead,' with nothing to the dead at all. . . . For if there was they couldn't all be candles and the effect would vanish. . . . And the elaborate, copious emptiness of the whole Henry James exploit is only redeemed and made endurable by the elaborate, copious wit. Upon the desert his selection has made Henry James 'erects palatial metaphors. . . . The chief fun, the only exercise, in reading Henry James is this clambering over vast metaphors. . . .

"Having first made sure that he has scarcely anything left to express, he then sets to work to express it, with an industry, a wealth of intellectual stuff that dwarfs Newton. He spares no resource in the telling of his dead inventions. He brings up every device of language to state and define. Bare verbs he rarely tolerates. He splits his infinitives and fills them up with adverbial stuffing. He presses the passing colloquialism into his service. His vast paragraphs sweat and struggle; they could not sweat and elbow and struggle more if God Himself was the processional meaning to which they sought to come. And all for tales of nothingness. . . . It is leviathan retrieving pebbles. It is a magnificent but painful hippopotamus resolved at any cost, even at the cost of its dignity, upon picking up a pea which has got into a corner of its den. Most things, it insists, are beyond it, but it can, at any rate, modestly, and with an artistic singleness of mind, pick up that pea. . . ."

§ 4

"A LITTLE while ago," said Boon, suddenly struggling with his trouser pocket and producing some pieces of paper, "I sketched out a novel, and as it was rather in the manner of Henry James I think perhaps you might be interested by it now. So much, that is, as there is of it. It is to be called 'The Spoils of Mr. Blandish,' and it is all about this particular business of the selective life. Mr. Blandish, as I saw him, was pretty completely taken from the James ideal. . . . He was a man with an exquisite apprehension of particulars, with just that sense of there being a rightness attainable, a fitness, a charm, a finish. . . . In any little affair. . . . He believed that in speech and still more that in writing there was an inevitable right word, in actions great and small a mellowed etiquette, in everything a possible perfection. He was, in fact, the very soul of Henry James—as I understand it. . . . This sort of man—

"Going delicately."

I was able to secure the sketch.

"He didn't marry, he didn't go upon adventures; lust, avarice, ambition, all these things that as Milton says are to be got 'not without dust and heat,' were not for him. Blood and dust and heat—he ruled them out. But he had independent means, he could live freely and delicately and charmingly, he could travel and meet and be delighted by all the best sorts of people in the best sorts of places. So for years he enriched his resonances, as an admirable violin grows richer with every note it sounds. He went about elaborately, avoiding ugliness, death, suffering, industrialism, politics, sport, the thought of war, the red blaze of passion. He travelled widely in the more settled parts of the world. Chiefly he visited interesting and ancient places, putting his ever more exquisite sensorium at them, consciously taking delicate impressions upon the refined wax of his being. In a manner most carefully occasional, he wrote. Always of faded places. His 'Ypres' was wonderful. His 'Bruges' and his 'Hour of Van Eyk' . . .

"Such," said Boon, "is the hero. The story begins, oh! quite in the James manner with——" He read—

" 'At times it seemed inaccessible, a thing beyond hope, beyond imagining, and then at times it became so concrete an imagination, a desire so specific, so nearly expressed, as to grow if not to the exact particulars of longitude and latitude, yet at any rate so far as county and district and atmosphere were concerned, so far indeed as an intuition of proximity was concerned, an intimation that made it seem at last at certain moments as if it could not possibly be very much farther than just round the corner or over the crest. . . .'

"But I've left a good bit of that to write up. In the book there will be pages and sheets of that sentence. The gist is that Mr. Blandish wants a house to live in and that he has an idea of the kind of house he wants. And the chapter, the long, unresting, progressing chapter, expands and expands; it never jumps you forward, it never lets you off, you can't skip and you can't escape, until there comes at last a culminating distension of statement in which you realize more and more clearly, until you realize it with the unforgettable certainty of a thing long fought for and won at last, that Mr. Blandish has actually come upon the house and with a vigour of decision as vivid as a flash of lightning in a wilderness of troubled clouds, as vivid indeed as the loud, sonorous bursting of a long blown bladder, has said '*This is it!*' On that '*This is it*' my chapter ends, with an effect of enormous relief, with something of the beautiful serenity that follows a difficult parturition.

"The story is born.

"And then we leap forward to possession.

" 'And here he was, in the warmest reality, in the very heart of the materialization of his dream——' He has, in fact, got the house. For a year or so from its first accidental discovery he had done nothing but just covet the house; too fearful of an overwhelming disappointment even to make a definite inquiry as to its accessibility. But he has, you will gather, taken apartments in the neighbourhood, thither he visits frequently, and almost every day when he walks abroad the coveted house draws him. It is in a little seaside place on the east coast, and the only available walks are along the shore or inland across the golf-links. Either path offers tempting digressions towards *it*. He comes to know it from a hundred aspects and under a thousand conditions of light and atmosphere. . . . And while still in the early stage he began a curious and delicious secret practice in relationship. You have heard of the Spaniard in love, in love with a woman he had seen but once, whom he might never see again, a princess, etiquette-defended, a goddess, and who yet, seeing a necklace that became her, bought it for the joy of owning something that was at least by fitness hers. Even so did Mr. Blandish begin to buy first one little article and then, the fancy growing upon him more and more, things, 'pieces' they call them, that were in the vein of Samphire House. And then came the day, the wonderful day, when as he took his afternoon feast of the eye, the door opened, some one came out towards him. . . .

"It was incredible. They were giving him tea with hot, inadvisable scones—but their hotness, their close heaviness, he accepted with a ready devotion, would have accepted had they been ten times as hot and close and heavy, not heedlessly, indeed, but gratefully, willingly paying his price for these astonishing revelations that without an effort, serenely, calmly, dropped in between her gentle demands whether he would have milk and her mild inquiries as to the exact quantity of sugar his habits and hygienic outlook demanded, that his hostess so casually made. These generous, heedless people were talking of departures, of abandonments, of, so they put it, selling the dear old place, if indeed any one could be found to buy a place so old and so remote and—she pointed her intention with a laugh—so very, very dear. Repletion of scones were a small price to pay for such a glowing, such an incredible gift of opportunity, thrust thus straight into the willing, amazed hands. . . .

"He gets the house. He has it done up. He furnishes it, and every article of furniture seems a stroke of luck too good to be true. And to crown it all I am going to write one of those long crescendo passages that James loves, a sentence, pages of it, of happy event linking to happy event until at last the incredible completion, a butler, unquestionably Early Georgian, respectability, competence equally unquestionable, a wife who could

cook, and cook well, no children, no thought or possibility of children, and to crown all, the perfect name—
Mutimer!

"All this you must understand is told retrospectively
as Blandish installs himself in Samphire House. It is told
to the refrain, 'Still, fresh every morning, came the persuasion "This is too good to be true." ' And as it is told,
something else, by the most imperceptible degrees, by a
gathering up of hints and allusions and pointing details,
gets itself told too, and that is the growing realization in
the mind of Blandish of a something extra, of something
not quite bargained for,—the hoard and the haunting.
About the house hangs a presence. . . .

"He had taken it at first as a mere picturesque accessory
to the whole picturesque and delightful wreathing of
association and tradition about the place, that there should
be this ancient flavour of the cutlass and the keg, this
faint aroma of buried doubloons and Stevensonian experiences. He had assumed, etc. . . . He had gathered,
etc. . . . And it was in the most imperceptible manner
that beyond his sense of these takings and assumptions
and gatherings there grew his perception that the delicate
quiver of appreciation, at first his utmost tribute to these
illegal and adventurous and sanguinary associations, was
broadening and strengthening, was, one hardly knew
whether to say developing or degenerating, into a
nervous reaction, more spinal and less equivocally agreeable, into the question, sensed rather than actually

thought or asked, whether in fact the place didn't in certain lights and certain aspects and at certain unfavourable moments come near to evoking the ghost—if such sorites are permissible in the world of delicate shades—of the ghost, of the ghost of a shiver—of *aversion.* . . .

"And so at page a hundred and fifty or thereabouts we begin to get into the story," said Boon.

"You wade through endless marshes of subtle intimation, to a sense of a Presence in Samphire House. For a number of pages you are quite unable to tell whether this is a ghost or a legend or a foreboding or simply old-fashioned dreams that are being allusively placed before you. But there is an effect piled up very wonderfully, of Mr. Blandish, obsessed, uneasy, watching furtively and steadfastly his guests, his callers, his domestics, continually asking himself. 'Do they note it? Are they feeling it?'

"We break at last into incidents. A young friend of the impossible name of Deshman helps evolve the story; he comes to stay; he seems to feel the influence from the outset, he cannot sleep, he wanders about the house. . . . Do others know? *Others?* . . . The gardener takes to revisiting the gardens after nightfall. He is met in the shrubbery with an unaccountable spade in his hand and answers huskily. Why should a gardener carry a spade? Why should he answer huskily? Why should the presence, the doubt, the sense of something else elusively in the air about them, become intensified at the encounter? Oh! conceivably of course in many places, but just *there*! As some sort of protection, it may be. . . . Then suddenly as Mr. Blandish sits at his lonely but beautifully served dinner he becomes aware for the first time of a change in Mutimer.

"Something told him in that instant that Mutimer also *knew*. . . .

"Deshman comes again with a new and disconcerting habit of tapping the panelling and measuring the thickness of the walls when he thinks no one is looking, and then a sister of Mr. Blandish and a friend, a woman, yet not so much a woman as a disembodied intelligence in a feminine costume with one of those impalpable relationships with Deshman that people have with one another in the world of Henry James, an association of shadows, an atmospheric liaison. Follow some almost sentenceless conversations. Mr. Blandish walks about the shrubbery with the friend, elaborately getting at it—whatever it is—and in front of them, now hidden by the yew hedges, now fully in view, walks Deshman with the married and settled sister of Mr. Blandish. . . .

" 'So,' said Mr. Blandish, pressing the point down towards the newly discovered sensitiveness, 'where we feel, he it seems *knows*.'

"She seemed to consider.

" 'He doesn't know completely,' was her qualification.

" 'But he has something—something tangible.'

" 'If he can make it tangible.'

"On that the mind of Mr. Blandish played for a time.

" 'Then it isn't altogether tangible yet?'

" 'It isn't tangible enough for him to go upon.'

" 'Definitely something.'

"Her assent was mutely concise.

" 'That we on our part——?'

"The *we* seemed to trouble her.

" 'He knows more than you do,' she yielded.

"The gesture, the half turn, the momentary halt in the paces of Mr. Blandish, plied her further.

" 'More, I think, than he has admitted—to any one.'

" 'Even to you?'

"He perceived an interesting wave of irritation. 'Even to me,' he had wrung from her, but at the price of all further discussion.

"Putting the thing crassly," said Boon, "Deshman has got wind of a hoard, of a treasure, of something—Heaven as yet only knows what something—buried, imbedded, in some as yet unexplained way incorporated with Samphire House. On the whole the stress lies rather on treasure, the treasure of smuggling, of longshore practices, of illegality on the high seas. And still clearer is it that the amiable Deshman wants to get at it without the participation of Mr. Blandish. Until the very end you are never quite satisfied why Deshman wants to get at it in so private a fashion. As the plot thickens you are played about between the conviction that Deshman wants the

R

stuff for himself and the firm belief of the lady that against the possible intervention of the Treasury, he wants to secure it for Mr. Blandish, to secure it at least generously if nefariously, lest perhaps it should fall under the accepted definition and all the consequent confiscations of treasure trove. And there are further beautiful subtleties as to whether she really believes in this more kindly interpretation of the refined but dubitable Deshman. . . . A friend of Deshman's, shameless under the incredible name of Mimbleton, becomes entangled in this thick, sweet flow of narrative—the James method of introducing a character always reminds me of going round with the lantern when one is treacling for moths. Mimbleton has energy. He presses. Under a summer dawn of delicious sweetness Mimbleton is found insensible on the croquet lawn by Mr. Blandish, who, like most of the characters in the narrative from first to last, has been unable to sleep. And at the near corner of the house, close to a never before remarked ventilator, is a hastily and inaccurately refilled excavation. . . .

"Then events come hurrying in a sort of tangled haste making sibyl-like gestures.

"At the doorway Mutimer appears—swaying with some profound emotion. He is still in his evening attire. He has not yet gone to bed. In spite of the dawn he carried a burning candle—obliquely. At the sight of his master he withdraws—backwards and with difficulty. . . .

"Then," said Boon, "I get my crowning chapter: the

breakfast, a peculiar *something*, something almost palpable in the atmosphere—Deshman hoarse and a little talkative, Mimbleton with a possibly nervous headache, husky also and demanding tea in a thick voice, Mutimer waiting uneasily, and Mr. Blandish, outwardly calm, yet noting every particular, thinking meanings into every word and movement, and growing more and more clear in his conviction that *Mutimer knows—knows everything*. . . .

"Book two opens with Mr. Blandish practically in possession of the facts. Putting the thing coarsely, the treasure is—1813 brandy, in considerable quantities bricked up in a disused cellar of Samphire House. Samphire House, instead of being the fine claret of a refuge Mr. Blandish supposed, is a loaded port. But of course in the novel we shall not put things coarsely, and for a long time you will be by no means clear what the 'spirit' is that Mr. Blandish is now resolved to exorcise. He is, in fact, engaged in trying to get that brandy away, trying to de-alcoholize his existence, trying—if one must put the thing in all the concrete crudity of his fundamental intention—to sell the stuff. . . .

"Now in real life you would just go and sell it. But people in the novels of Henry James do not do things in the inattentive, offhand, rather confused, and partial way of reality: they bring enormous brains to bear upon the minutest particulars of existence. Mr. Blandish, following the laws of that world, has not simply to sell his brandy: he has to sell it subtly, intricately, interminably, with a delicacy, with a dignity. . . .

"He consults friends—impalpable, intricate, inexhaustible friends.

"There are misunderstandings. One old and trusted intimate concludes rather hastily that Mr. Blandish is confessing that he has written a poem, another that he is making a proposal of marriage, another that he wishes an introduction to the secretary of the Psychical Research Society. . . . "All this," said Boon, "remains, perhaps indefinitely, to be worked out. Only the end, the end, comes with a rush. Deshman has found for him—one never gets nearer to it than the 'real right people.' The real right people send their agent down, a curious blend of gentleman and commercial person he is, to investigate, to verify, to estimate quantities. Ultimately he will—shall we say it?—make an offer. With a sense of immense culmination the reader at last approaches the hoard. . . .

"You are never told the thing exactly. It is by indefinable suggestions, by exquisite approaches and startings back, by circumlocution the most delicate, that your mind at last shapes its realization, that—the last drop of the last barrel has gone and that Mutimer, the butler, lies dead or at least helpless—in the inner cellar. And a beautiful flavour, ripe and yet rare, rich without opulence, hangs—*diminuendo morendo*—in the air. . . ."

68

JAMES TO WELLS

21 *Carlyle Mansions,*
Cheyne Walk, S.W.
July 6th, 1915.

MY DEAR WELLS.

I was given yesterday at a club your volume *Boon,*
etc., from a loose leaf in which I learn that you kindly
sent it me and which yet appears to have lurked there for
a considerable time undelivered. I have just been reading, to acknowledge it intelligently, a considerable number of its pages—though not all; for, to be perfectly
frank, I have been in that respect beaten for the first time
—or rather for the first time but one—by a book of
yours: I haven't found the current of it draw me on and
on this time—as unfailingly and irresistibly before (which
I have repeatedly let you know.) However, I shall try
again—I hate to lose any scrap of you that *may* make for
light or pleasure; and meanwhile I have more or less
mastered your appreciation of H. J., which I have found
very curious and interesting, after a fashion—though it
has naturally not filled me with a fond elation. It is difficult of course for a writer to put himself *fully* in the place
of another writer who finds him extraordinarily futile and
void, and who is moved to publish that to the world—

and I think the case isn't easier when he happens to have
enjoyed the other writer enormously, from far back; because there has then grown up the habit of taking some
common meeting-ground between them for granted, and
the falling away of this is like the collapse of a bridge
which made communication possible. But I am by nature
more in dread of any fool's paradise, or at least of any
bad misguidedness, than in love with the idea of a
security proved, and the fact that a mind as brilliant as
yours *can* resolve me into such an unmitigated mistake,
can't enjoy me in anything like the degree in which I like
to think I may be enjoyed, makes me greatly want to fix
myself, for as long as my nerves will stand it, with such a
pair of eyes. I am aware of certain things I have, and not
less conscious, I believe, of various others that I am simply reduced to wish I did or could have; so I try, for
possible light, to enter into the feelings of a critic for
whom the deficiencies so preponderate. The difficulty
about that effort, however, is that one can't keep it up—
one *has* to fall back on one's sense of one's good parts—
one's own sense; and I at least should have to do that, I
think, even if your picture were painted with a more
searching brush. For I should otherwise seem to forget
what it is that my poetic and my appeal to experience rest
upon. They rest upon *my* measure of fulness—fulness of
life and of the projection of it, which seems to you such
an emptiness of both. I don't mean to say I don't wish I
could do twenty things I can't—many of which you do so

livingly; but I confess I ask myself what would become in that case of some of those to which I am most addicted and by which interest seems to me most beautifully producible. I hold that interest may be, *must* be, exquisitely made and created, and that if we don't make it, we who undertake to, nobody and nothing will make it for us; though nothing is more possible, nothing may even be more certain, than that my quest of it, my constant wish to run it to earth, may entail the sacrifice of certain things that are not on the straight line of it. However, there are too many things to say, and I don't think your chapter is really inquiring enough to entitle you to expect all of them. The fine thing about the fictional form to me is that it opens such widely different windows of attention; but that is just why I like the window so to frame the play and the process!

Faithfully yours

HENRY JAMES

69

WELLS TO JAMES

July 8th 1915

MY DEAR JAMES,

You write me so kind and frank a letter after my offences that I find it an immense embarrassment to reply to you. I have set before myself a gamin-esque ideal, I have a natural horror of dignity, finish and perfection, a horror a little enhanced by theory. You may take it that my sparring and punching at you is very much due to the feeling that you were "coming over" me, and that if I was not very careful I should find myself giving way altogether to respect. There is of course a real and very fundamental difference in our innate and developed attitudes towards life and literature. To you literature like painting is an end, to me literature like architecture is a means, it has a use. Your view was, I felt, altogether too dominant in the world of criticism, and I assailed it in tones of harsh antagonism. And writing that stuff about you was the first escape I had from the obsession of this war. *Boon* is just a waste-paper basket. Some of it was written before I left my house at Sandgate, and it was while I was turning over some old papers that I came upon it, found it expressive and went on with it last December. I had rather be called a journalist than an artist, that is the essence of it, and there was no other antagonist possible than yourself. But since it was printed I have regretted a hundred times that I did not express our profound and incurable difference and contrast with a better grace. And believe me, my dear James, your very keenly appreciative reader, your warm if rebellious and resentful admirer, and for countless causes yours most gratefully and affectionately

H. G. Wells

70

JAMES TO WELLS

21 *Carlyle Mansions,*
Cheyne Walk, S.W.
July 10*th*, 1915.

[*Dictated.*]

MY DEAR WELLS.

I am bound to tell you that I don't think your letter
makes out any sort of case for the bad manners of *Boon,*
so far as your indulgence in them at the expense of your
poor old H. J. is concerned—I say "your" simply because he has *been* yours, in the most liberal, continual,
sacrificial, the most admiring and abounding critical way,
ever since he began to know your writings: as to which
you have had copious testimony. Your comparison of
the book to a waste-basket strikes me as the reverse of
felicitous, for what one throws into that receptacle is
exactly what one *doesn't* commit to publicity and make
the affirmation of one's estimate of one's contemporaries
by. I should liken it much rather to the preservative port-
folio or drawer in which what is withheld from the basket
is savingly laid away. Nor do I feel it anywhere evident
that my "view of life and literature," or what you impute
to me as such, is carrying everything before it and becoming a public menace—so unaware do I seem, on the
contrary, that my products constitute an example in any

measurable degree followed or a cause in any degree successfully pleaded: I can't but think that if this were the
case I should find it somewhat attested in their circula-
tion—which, alas, I have reached a very advanced age in
the entirely defeated hope of. But I *have* no view of life
and literature, I maintain, other than that our form of the
latter in especial is admirable exactly by its range and
variety, its plasticity and liberality, its fairly living on the
sincere and shifting experience of the individual practitioner. That is why I have always so admired your so
free and strong application of it, the particular rich receptacle of intelligences and impressions emptied out with
an energy of its own, that your genius constitutes; and
that is in particular why, in my letter of two or three days
since, I pronounced it curious and interesting that you
should find the case I constitute myself only ridiculous
and vacuous to the extent of your having to proclaim
your sense of it. The curiosity and the interest, however,
in this latter connection are of course for my mind those
of the break of perception (perception of the vivacity of
my variety) on the part of a talent so generally inquiring
and apprehensive as yours. Of course for myself I live,
live intensely and am fed by life, and my value, whatever
it be, is in my own kind of expression of that. Therefore
I am pulled up to wonder by the fact that for you my
kind (my sort of sense of expression and sort of sense of
life alike) doesn't exist; and that wonder is, I admit, a disconcerting comment on my idea of the various appre-

ciability of our addiction to the novel and of all the personal and intellectual history, sympathy and curiosity, behind the given example of it. It is when that history and curiosity have been determined in the way most different from my own that I myself want to get at them —precisely *for* the extension of life, which is the novel's best gift. But that is another matter. Meanwhile I absolutely dissent from the claim that there are any differences whatever in the amenability to art of forms of literature aesthetically determined, and hold your distinction between a form that is (like) painting and a form that is (like) architecture for wholly null and void. There is no sense in which architecture is aesthetically "for use" that doesn't leave any other art whatever exactly as much so; and so far from that of literature being irrelevant to the literary report upon life, and to its being made as interesting as possible, I regard it as relevant in a degree that leaves everything else behind. It is art that *makes* life, makes interest, makes importance, for our consideration and application of these things, and I know of no substitute whatever for the force and beauty of its process.[1]

[1] Percy Lubbock in *The Letters of Henry James* (2 volumes, New York, 1920, II, 488) quotes the following sentences from a letter of Wells to James dated July 13, 1915, the full text of which has not survived: "I don't clearly understand your concluding phrases—which shews no doubt how completely they define our difference. When you say 'it is art that *makes* life, makes interest, makes importance,' I can only read sense into it by assuming that you are using 'art' for every conscious human activity. I use the word for a research and attainment that is technical and special."

If I were Boon I should say that any pretence of such a substitute is helpless and hopeless humbug; but I wouldn't be Boon for the world, and am only yours faithfully

HENRY JAMES

INDEX